THE VIEW FROM STERLING BLUFF

THE VIEW FROM STERLING BLUFF

From General Oglethorpe to Henry Ford to Today

———————————

WRITTEN BY
GLEN McCASKEY

PHOTOGRAPHY
BILL WEEMS
STEVE UZZELL

LONGSTREET PRESS
ATLANTA

Published by
LONGSTREET PRESS, INC.
2150 Newmarket Parkway
Suite 102
Marietta, Georgia 30067

Printed in the United States of America

1st Printing, 1988

Library of Congress Catalog Card Number 88-083080

ISBN 0-929264-13-4

TABLE OF CONTENTS

INTRODUCTION

Henry Ford is still a contemporary benchmark for those who live along the Ogeechee. As the river meanders peacefully into Georgia's coastal tidelands, events there start to be dated with the Ford era in view; "Now before Henry . . ." "Of course, that was after Mister Ford came and . . ."

The Henry Ford story at Richmond Hill, Georgia is a fascinating one but it is in good company. This tranquil land abounded in gripping stories for 200 years before the Fords added their intriguing dimension to the picture. Men of remarkable vision and talent were attracted here before Ford and this book briefly considers their struggles and exploits.

The first landmark on the Ogeechee mentioned by the early settlers happened to be but a few stone throws from where Henry Ford would build his great mansion. It was called "Sterling Bluff" and it is from Sterling Bluff that this view of Henry Ford in Georgia, his predecessors and his successors shall be taken.

The View will take time to feast on the banquet of plantation history along the river. The tumultuous sights of the Revolutionary War and the grand days thereafter will be unveiled. The Civil War and the incumbent valor and agony are part of another scene.

The View from the old bluff will look closely at Henry Ford. He came to coastal Georgia unexpectedly. He did unexpected things. He left it a remarkably different place. He became part of the place and the people.

Other people, communities and even nations around the world wanted him, sought him. The Chinese government asked Ford to become its economic advisor. Germany's Finance Minister tried to persuade him to become the "Economic Dictator" of that country and a wing of Polish monarchists wanted Ford to assume their country's throne.

He did not accept any of those modest offers. Ford was a man who did as he liked. He liked a place none of those power brokers had ever heard of, a struggling little community on a tranquil river in Georgia that never would have thought even to extend Ford an invitation to visit.

Richmond Hill, Georgia won a race with China, Germany, Poland and a host of other places without ever knowing it was in a race. It was to this little whistle-stop town that the great Henry Ford would commit himself, his resources, and his ingenuity. It was a largely unheralded commitment. But it was appreciated along the Ogeechee.

"Henry Ford came here providentially," was what the local people said. They loved Henry Ford. He cared. He took a tired land and tilled it. He took a largely defeated, hopeless people and gave them opportunity for personal victory and a hope that began to reflect his own remarkable outlook.

The Ford era returned the land along the Ogeechee River to the vitality that had characterized it during those previous generations. Henry Ford in the long view from Sterling Bluff was much like other men who also had been drawn to what was called the Ogeechee Neck. Those other men included Indians, European settlers and the Southern planters. Why some of them came here was not easy to understand either.

Perhaps it was the enticing sparkle of the river with its deep water and abundant shad population. The twisted and majestic oaks added both beauty and the desired shapes for ships' keels in the earliest days. The land was good and the lowlands perfect for rice. Wildlife was abundant.

The vista along the river was and is remarkable. Over a century ago men were writing with awe about the ancient oaks at Richmond Plantation. What would they say now that thirteen additional decades have been added to those majestic trees. The natural beauty here has but one rival – the historical beauty.

Whatever it was that drew people like Henry Ford to the shores of the Ogeechee, the land today is layered with the relics of those historic and prehistoric populations. Future generations will come, too. It is the intention of the following words and pictures to enable both passersby, native and future settlers, to more deeply delight in the remarkable View from Sterling Bluff.

1
INDIANS AND EUROPEANS

History is made up of the blending of some pretty remarkable currents of life and nature. The story in the tidal part of Georgia called the Ogeechee Neck is one of the most intriguing blends found anywhere. It contains paradoxes, happenings and surprises that one does not soon forget. It is a story which spans centuries but does not fade in its fascination.

The men and women in this story were vital people, innovative, bold and spirited. Maybe the Ogeechee attracts people like that. Henry Ford would wrestle with munitions manufacturers, labor unions and malaria while his predecessors along the Ogeechee River would wrangle with smugglers, Indians, Spaniards, Tory Englishmen and civil war. The men and women involved in the struggles, though spanning centuries, indeed had a great deal in common. Their character, respect for the land along the River and attitudes toward one another almost made them look as if they had been poured from one mold.

The View From Sterling Bluff is a long view. Great volumes of water have flowed past its serene setting as has a proportionate share of drama. The river is quieter now than when it used to be one of two main arteries of transportation into the Georgia frontier. Thousands of men have come and gone but men still fish for shad in the passing waters. Things are different but things are much the same as well, as the View From Sterling Bluff reveals.

Before the Invasion

This land was a very popular place with American Indians. Artifacts from archaeology on the property bear abundant evidence to the prehistoric popularity of the shores along the Ogeechee. Here were lands easily accessed by canoe, offering an abundance of wildlife and good soil for growing maize, melons, potatoes, pumpkins and other Indian crops. Henry Ford would try to "grow" his Ford cars here.

The Indians here were called the "Creeks" by the Europeans because they lived along the creeks and small waterways of the coastal region. The Creeks called themselves Este Muskokee, ranging as a loosely organized nation from Florida to the Carolinas. A small tribe called the Yamacraws were here, too.

A Yamacraw chief named Tomochichi is credited with having granted Georgia founder General James Oglethorpe the land for the establishment of nearby Savannah, only 23 miles from what is now Richmond Hill. Oglethorpe described his Indian benefactors as follows:

> "The men paint themselves red, blue, yellow and black," he wrote. "The women wear a petticoat to the knees. Their shoes are a kind of pump made of deerskin, called a moccasin. They have plenty of Indian corn, pumpkins, potatoes, mushmelons, watermelons, peas, peaches, plums, nectarines and fowls and hogs in abundance. They use the fat of the bear for oil and honey combs for sugar."

It was from Ford's Island (left) that a bear once charged early settlers along the Ogeechee.

Savannah's River Street on a quiet afternoon along the Savannah River.

The original town plan for Savannah was faithfully executed and substantially survives today.

Long before the Englishman Oglethorpe would come to the Georgia coast, the Spanish had spent several generations in the area, long enough that they came to look upon it as their own. Pedro de Quexos was the first known European to come ashore in the area. He did so in 1521 at a spot he called La Punta de Santa Elena. This has been diversely pinpointed as Tybee Island, Georgia, Georgetown, South Carolina and numerous places in between. A settlement was established there in 1525 with 500 colonists but it failed within a year due to disease and internal dissension.

The French also came through in 1562 under the direction of Jean Ribaut who established a settlement a few miles north of the Savannah River in Port Royal Sound. Every time these French Huguenots encountered a Georgia river, they named it after a river in France. The Ogeechee River was named either the Bellum or the Gironde.

It was the Spanish, however, who endured in Georgia. They established garrisons and missions from Florida to South Carolina with a later version Santa Elena having a sizable town of over 60 houses by 1580. The English started to rattle their sabers around that time and with the 1586 attack of Sir Francis Drake on the Spanish North American capital of St. Augustine, Florida, the Spanish pulled back their more exposed garrisons, including those in South Carolina and Georgia. Even so, missions of the Catholic Church remained active for another 80 years.

The English started pressing the Spanish advantage in Georgia with the establishment of Charleston, South Carolina in 1670. They would have settled further South had it not been for the Spanish threat from Florida, which at that time included what would become "Georgia."

By 1701 the English had established a lookout post with palisade, watch tower and quarters within sight of Georgia on what is now the southernmost inhabited island in South Carolina, Daufuskie Island. This mini-fortress was the southern frontier point of all English Colonial government in North America. The purpose of the post was to guard against not only the Spanish, but also the Indians of Florida who had been enlisted as Spanish allies against the encroaching English.

The first Anglican attempt to colonize Georgia was made in 1717 when Scotsman Sir Robert Montgomery obtained a Royal Charter from the Savannah River to the Altamaha. He was greatly enraptured by the land and called it the "Margravate of Azilia." Not being a man given to understatement, Montgomery termed it "the most delightful country in the universe" but he failed to colonize it within the prescribed time and lost his charter to such a remarkable place.

Savannah Settled

On June 9, 1732, the Crown of England passed Sir Robert's charter on to another group of "Trustees" administered by General James Oglethorpe. The boundaries were the same but ranging westerly all the way to the Pacific and eastward 20 leagues into the Atlantic. The economic basis of the colony was to be founded on the manufacture of silk and wine, both of which would fail.

The establishment of the new colony, the last of the original 13, was rooted on both idealism and practicality. A member of Parliament, General Oglethorpe was a crusader against the loathsome conditions of English debtor's prisons and thus sought to give the debtor a new chance in life by immigration to Georgia. Practically, the other colonies, particularly South Carolina, saw in the creation of the Colony of Georgia an opportunity to stabilize the Indian and Spanish threat from the South by letting the Georgians be a buffer.

On February 12, 1733, General Oglethorpe and 114 colonists arrived from Gravesend, England in what is now the prosperous international seaport of Savannah. They came on the good ship ANN to Charleston and traveled to Yamacraw Bluff on the Savannah River via smaller craft. There Oglethorpe laid out Georgia's first planned city in blocks of five symmetrical 60 x 90 foot lots. A system of public squares, still prominent in the old city, was created for purposes of both fortification in case of attack as well as social interaction. Each family received a house lot on one of the squares and a five acre garden plot outside of the city, with 45 acre farm plots available still further out.

Oglethorpe had lofty aspirations for the new colony named in honor of King George II. Initially he barred slavery, rum and lawyers from Georgia, seeing all three as contrary to the best interests of the new English settlement. Henry Ford would later reflect very similar sentiments. Both men were social experimenters in Georgia.

Within time, all three of these "scourges" would infect Oglethorpe's experiment and bring about substantial conflict. During the time he was able to prevent the influx of these vices, Oglethorpe proceeded to make peace with the Indians, barter more land from them and begin to establish defenses around the new colony. He reduced the threat of Spanish attack from St. Augustine with a series of military engagements and rather quickly created an environment conducive to frontier styled settlement.

After one year of settlement, colonists from Savannah were branching out into such not so distant regions as the nearby Ogeechee Neck, lands located between the great Ogeechee River on the north, the Midway and

Old rice field canals like this one at Sterling Bluff still survive along the Ogeechee River.

Tomochichi was the Indian chief who welcomed General Oglethorpe to what is now Savannah, Georgia.

Jerico Rivers on the south and St. Catherine Sound to the east. Oglethorpe was granting estates of up to 2,000 acres and he had definite standards for those who wanted these free lands: "trustees do not propose to subsist any people in the colony who do not cultivate land for their own subsistence." In other words, those "colonizing" Georgia would have to be self-supporting or lose their property. Ford would also come proclaiming a doctrine of self-sufficiency.

Much like the settlements of Australia and Alaska in more recent times, the potential for free land was widely heralded in Britain and enterprises were established specifically for bringing settlers to the 13th American colony. Here, too, special interest groups, such as Christian communities seeking life apart from the restrictions of Europe's state controlled churches, found the opportunities in Georgia appealing.

The Sterling Brothers

One of the earliest grants made by Oglethorpe outside of Savannah was to two brothers from Scotland. In 1734 Hugh and William Sterling were granted an estate of probably 2,000 acres on the Ogeechee River at a spot called "Sterling Bluff." The brothers did not remain long at their newly acquired property, although some of it remained in the family for many years. The Sterlings attracted the attention of the Georgia trustees in ways that apparently led to the revoking of a portion of their original grant.

First, William Sterling was fined for having an illegitimate child via a servant. Next Hugh Sterling carried a petition directly to the trustees in England and asked that the colonists be allowed to import slaves, a request that was "resented" by the trustees as an "insult to their honor." Finally, in 1737, after an initial commendation for successful clearing and planting, the scandalous fact was reported that the "Scotch gentlemen named Sterlings have left their plantation upon the Ogeechee River and taken house in Savannah."

This was a despicable state of affairs in the new colony because the whole purpose of the land grants was to bring the land into cultivation and provide export to England. The Sterlings were not living up to their end of the bargain. Having freely taken 2,000 acres, they were not being self-supporting at all but rather were sitting in a rented house in Savannah living off the labors of others. As Resident Secretary of the Georgia Trustees, William Stephens reported to his supervisors in 1737:

> Landholders make great professions of good will to the colony and give ready obedience to the civil power, but complain of their losses in improving land, the precariousness of their tenures . . .
>
> Chief among these are: Andrew Grant, setler at Ogychee, and the two brethren, Hugh and William Sterling, at Ogychee, Scotchmen.
>
> Grant quitted his land at Ogychie and brought away all his servants; tho' he has no employment for 'em in town, where he lives.
>
> The two brothers Sterlings have done the same thing and their servants lie on their hands here in town where they rent a house; and bake bread, or turn their hands to what else they can, rather than work farther on their lands; which indeed I am most surpryzed at; because when I was last here, there were none in the whole province more celebrated for the large quantity of land they had cleared and planted.

Why would anyone abandon a free plantation on the serenely flowing Ogeechee River? What was wrong with these troublesome Scotsmen?

Plantation life in Georgia in 1737 was something less than an earlier version of "Gone with the Wind." It was a difficult and still somewhat dangerous existence, although General Oglethorpe probably had made the settlement of the colony safer than any of the other twelve at this stage of development.

Men often went to church armed for fear of the remaining Indians who both traded with the settlers and stole from them. The Ogeechee Neck had been as popular with the natives as it was becoming with the intruding Europeans. The large Indian mounds still existing in Bryan County bear continuing testimony to the fact that the Creek and other tribes lived here.

The houses of the settlers were generally framed and weather-boarded with clay chimneys. They were normally one story with four rooms and perhaps a loft accessible by ladder for storage or small children. What quality of life there was along the river was often interrupted by alarms of Indian raids or rumors of Spanish and even French incursions.

Bear Country

It was into this kind of setting that a band of Moravians made their visit to Sterling Bluff around 1735. Dispatched by the well known German religious reformer Nikolaus Ludwig Count Von Zinzedorf, the missionary minded Moravians were on their way up the Ogeechee to inspect lands granted to them near one of Oglethorpe's defensive outposts, the wooden stockaded Fort Argyle. Under the leadership of Gottlieb Spangenberg, "the Moravian party spent the night at Sterling's Bluff with the Scotch who had settled upon it, and then the next morning they proceeded to Fort Argyle."

It was here that a bear left one of the islands in the river, probably the one now named Ford's Island, and swam across towards the travelers. The historical records show that the Moravians' official game keeper for the expedition, Peter Rose, took two shots at the bear but missed. Such were the joys of plantation life in those early days.

The Moravians in Georgia would play an unexpectedly important role in the history of Great Britain as it would be through this same band that a troubled Anglican missionary to the colony, John Wesley, would come to grips with the absence of his own "conversion." Wesley would soon return to England and ignite the First Great Evangelical Awakening that headed off an English version of the disastrous French Revolution.

Wesley, whose brother Charles was secretary to General Oglethorpe, came to the colony in 1736 on the same boat with Spangenberg's band of Moravian families. In crossing the stormy Atlantic, the boat passed through a terrible tempest which found Wesley cowered by anguish while the Moravians, "including the children," said Wesley, met "total deliverance from the spirit of fear." Wesley would cry out later, "I went to Georgia to convert the Indians, but oh, who shall convert me?" The answer was provided by the Moravian brethren who stayed in Georgia until 1740 when they packed up and moved north to Pennsylvania.

A Wealthier Class

In 1741, eight years after the settlement of Savannah, a new influx of colonists came to Georgia, a group that was very pleasing to the trustees because of their wealth and reputation. These were not men such as the Sterling brothers, men who could not be counted on, but "substantial citizens." One of the most notable was John Harn, the grantee of the estate where Henry Ford would build his beautiful winter home.

The first 500 acres of the grant were given to Harn on October 29, 1748. The site is just up river from Sterling Bluff where the Ogeechee makes a sharp turn from the west and curves back into the southwest at a high bank now adorned with moss-draped live oaks. It was there that John Harn would establish himself in the view of the trustees as, "sufficient in both ability and industry." These words would be an apt description of subsequent stewards of this estate and particularly one named Henry Ford.

Harn named his colonial holdings Dublin Plantation, probably after an ancestral home. He had emigrated to the New World around 1731 from Scotland and lived in Maryland and South Carolina before settling in Georgia. He participated in the 1740 attack on St. Augustine from South Carolina which may have won him his grant in Georgia. Many of the grants along the Ogeechee went to those who had so served the cause of "English justice" in America. Captain Mackay would end up with Strathy Hall on the other side of Sterling Bluff this way and Captain Demere would build nearby at White Hall Plantation.

Around 1747, John Harn packed up his wife, Elizabeth, his nine children, his 28 slaves (Oglethorpe's ban on slavery was about to be reversed) and moved into his new Dublin Plantation. It is safe to assume that Harn was the one responsible for planting the now massive live oaks at the site of his plantation in the shape of the letter "H." Harn would soon begin expanding his holdings with Sterling Bluff and the Cherry Hill Plantation site as part of the substantial growth pattern which would characterize the Harns in Georgia.

2
RICE, ROYALTY AND REBELLION

Statues stand in Savannah's historic squares today, this one of Georgia's founder, General James Oglethorpe.

A significant number of prominent South Carolinians like the Harns were emigrating to the new colony of Georgia around the same time Dublin Plantation was established. The reasons were several. First, the trustees were not entirely delighted with the caliber of the "new blood" they had been able to recruit from the British Isles or other colonies. According to Georgia historian Hugh McCall:

> Georgia continued to be an asylum for insolvent and embarrassed debtors from Carolina and the other colonies, which added to the indolence that had previously prevailed and kept the colony sunk in insignificance and contempt.

Secondly, many people who had moved to the new colony did not have hands-on experience with rice cultivation. The new wave of South Carolinians did.

Thirdly, the South Carolinians had slaves, which were still illegal from an import standpoint in Georgia. What often happened during the days before the trustees changed their position was that Georgia planters would rent South Carolina slaves from their owners or even rent them from themselves if they had moved into Georgia. There was also some "licensing" of slaves by the trustees before they opened the gate to the woeful institution.

The colony reached a crisis on the issue when the time of indenture for the first wave of indentured servants from England started to expire. Planters soon found themselves without common laborers. This left few acceptable options other than hiring slaves from other colonies or defying the law. To continue without slavery would have launched the economy onto a totally different course.

The demand for slavery grew until finally, in 1747, a public meeting was called in Savannah to discuss the question. Ogeechee Neck grantees were substantially represented. In spite of vigorous opposition by Scottish and German settlers, an agreement was struck so that in 1751 the trustees allowed slavery into Georgia with strict restrictions. For example,

> Owners of slaves should educate the young and use every possible means of making religious impressions upon the minds of the aged, and that all acts of inhumanity should be punished by the civil authority.

Legislation would later be passed which would counter these and other good measures. While still prohibiting cruelty to slaves, it would further disenfranchise them.

South Carolina also played a role in the reversal of General Oglethorpe's edict on rum. Such a vigorous rum smuggling operation was operated out of nearby Daufuskie Island that Oglethorpe had to set up a border patrol to keep the contraband from being transported into the colony via the Savannah and Ogeechee Rivers. At one point, Oglethorpe even threatened to forcibly annex the South Carolina island in order to stem the influx of rum.

Another basic tenet of General Oglethorpe's plans that did not work out was the silk industry. The Europeans could not get the thought of silk out of their minds. That notion had lingered since the very first explorations in search of new routes to India and China. The Virginians had tried to grow silk in Williamsburg and had failed miserably and the same would happen in Georgia.

All that remains of Silk Hope Plantation on the Ogeechee today is its now tangled and massive live oak promenade.

Kilted General Oglethorpe shows his political skill as he visits Scottish settlers.

Sunsets along the Ogeechee tidelands during plantation days would have included barges laden with rice. (Right)

Silk exports between 1750 and 1754 generated $8,897 for the colony. In 1757, only 1,050 pounds of silk were exported, rising to around 10,000 pounds in 1759. Still the industry never succeeded and with the change in slavery laws, the economy turned increasingly to rice. Soon Sea Island Cotton would play an important role while indigo and lumber exports would continue to be steady generators of revenue.

Dead Towns and Royal Governors

Life along the Ogeechee became easier as a result of the new slavery laws, easier for the gentlemen slave owners that is, those who enjoyed social events, hunting and fishing while their slaves tilled the fields or occasionally served as rowing crews for the planters' periodic crew races on the Ogeechee and Midway Rivers. The "rowing sports" would continue among the black population until Henry Ford's time, with black employees staging bateaux races for the auto magnate and rowing tug-of-war contests that often resulted in snapped oars.

Much of the social life of the period, when knee-buckles and powdered wigs were in vogue, found expression in the fine homes that were increasingly rising along the Ogeechee and throughout the Neck. The trustees were gone and a Royal Governor was reigning over the Colony by that time. Inevitably the King's representatives seemed to end up with their own estates among the plantations granted to the veterans of Spanish and Indian conflicts and this especially encouraged planters moving in from other colonies. Some became involved in the town of Hardwicke, which today is classified as one of the "dead towns" of Georgia.

Hardwicke was the brainchild of such men as John Harn of Dublin, Captain Mackay of Strathy Hall, associates of Oglethorpe and other wealthy planters. The idea behind Hardwicke was to build another planned city in Georgia, but this time on the lower part of the Ogeechee River, about 12 miles south of the present Richmond Hill. "It would be of great service to the province and the British nation to have a dockyard and settlements on the river which is capacious enough to contain some hundred sail of ships from seventy guns downward" read a memorial written by proponent Joseph Avery as early as 1741.

Another benefit of the site was that it was above the tide line and thus offered fresh water to ocean going vessels, allowing them to "lie secure from the worms, as the river is always fresh at the elbow . . ." Interestingly, the salty tideline today extends around 13 miles further inland than in that day. The site also was seen to offer a much more convenient seaport for the export of rice, indigo and lumber being shipped out from the Neck.

The town was laid out somewhat along the lines of Savannah and named George Town for the King. The first Royal Governor, John Reynolds, visited the town in 1755 and renamed it Hardwicke in honor of his relative, Lord Hardwicke, Lord High Chancellor of England.

Governor Reynolds and his royal successor, Governor Henry Ellis, both wanted to move the capital from Savannah to Hardwicke, to the extent that "development of Savannah was allowed to lag and the city fall into a sad state of repair." Funds, however, were not forthcoming for the project and while the city did reach a population of around 100, the transfer of the capital never took place and the next Royal Governor, Sir James Wright, threw a damper on turning the site into the major trading village the entrepreneurial Ogeechee planters envisioned.

Hardwicke advocate Governor Reynolds was recalled to England to face charges of inefficiency and impropriety. When his successor Henry Ellis arrived in Savannah in February, 1757, he was greeted at the docks with cheers by the citizens. He too would quickly become financially involved in Hardwicke and became anything but an asset to the new colony. Royal Governor Ellis, it seems, fancied himself a gentlemen's gentleman. He did not like warm climates. "The inhabitants of Savannah," thought he "breathed a hotter air than any other people on earth."

Historian McCall reports scenes of the Governor walking around town greatly incensed by the heat. Often he would venture out of doors in the heat of the day with an open umbrella to protect his sensitivities from the Georgia sun. Suspended inside the umbrella by a thread "as high as his face" was a thermometer that would confirm his very worst suspicions about the temperature. In 1759, Governor Ellis requested permission to return to England because his health was giving way to the heat. His request was granted, much to the joy of the people he governed.

His successor would be the most popular Royal Governor and ironically, the one that would be in office when the American Revolution would begin in Georgia. Governor James Wright was actually born in Charleston, South Carolina although he was educated in England. He had a long-time familiarity with the cultivation of rice and within 20 years became known as the "richest Tory in the province" because of his more than a dozen plantations on the Ogeechee Neck.

The Tide of Revolution

Governor Wright's popularity would delay the revolution in Georgia but it could not prevent it. A growing spirit of discontent was festering in the colony over the insensitivities of the British to the needs and circumstances of the populace. The famous Stamp Act of 1765, passed by the home government to support the English army in the Colonies, was the last straw for

Slavery was initially barred from Georgia by its founders.

many, although there were also a good many loyal Englishmen among the Ogeechee River plantation owners.

The stamp tax legislation was repealed the next year but not before riots had taken place in Savannah and the governor burned in effigy. Peace would return until the next wave of English taxes but the victory for the colonists and the adversarial relationship between some of them and the mother country foretold further conflict. In 1771 Governor Wright would sail for England to return as Sir James in 1773. An Ogeechee River planter, James Habersham, Secretary of the Colony was acting governor in his absence.

In January 1775, a provincial congress was called in Georgia to discuss the movement toward liberty. In May, a party of young patriots, led by Secretary Habersham's second son, Joseph, broke into the powder magazine at the eastern edge of Savannah and took away 600 pounds of gun powder. Some was kept in Georgia, the rest was sent secretly to South Carolina and on to New England where it was used by patriots in the Battle of Bunker Hill.

In June of that same year, while the Tories were celebrating the King's birthday, a party of patriots spiked the cannon in the battery in Savannah and dumped them over the bluff into the river. Royalist soldiers retrieved the guns and redrilled them amidst great hooting from the populace, the whole affair being followed by a defiant and noisy parade through town.

The advent of war in Georgia in 1776 created enormous personal and economic difficulties for the colonists, most of whom had only been there one or two decades. Typical of the dilemmas faced by many families was that of the Habersham family, which had holdings on the Neck but lived on the Little Ogeechee River. Head of the family, James Habersham came to Georgia from England at 26 and became a powerful influence in the establishment of the colony. Initially heading one of Oglethorpe's military troops, he went on to oversee industrial development of the colony, focusing first on silk and then later raising and exporting the first cotton from Savannah.

When the smoke of rebellion filled the air, Habersham was sympathetic with the people but he also believed in obeying his king. As an officer of the crown, he felt bound to remain loyal. His three sons, however, became ardent patriots of the Revolution. The younger James Habersham took the Royal Governor prisoner on January 18, 1776 after independence was declared. John and Joseph became members of the Continental Congress and Joseph went on to become speaker of the State General Assembly and postmaster under George Washington. Mercifully for the family, the elder Habersham died in 1775 and was thus spared the heart-rending days of the war.

The Tattnalls of Belvedere and Kilkenny plantations were not so fortunate. The elder Tattnall was also an ardent Loyalist while his son, Josiah Tattnall, Jr., was a staunch patriot. The elder man's properties were confiscated by the revolutionaries in the Georgia Act of Attainder in 1778 and in the Act of Confiscation and Banishment of 1782.

The son went on to become Governor of the new state of Georgia and in 1801, almost 20 years after the war, the state legislature passed a special act repealing the banishment of the elder Tattnall. Signing the act as governor, Josiah Tattnall, Jr. wrote, "With lively impression of gratitude, I affix my signature to this act, the 4th of Dec., 1801."

Hardships of the War

Confiscation of property along the Ogeechee was like a tennis match. It went back and forth as first the British were in control, then the patriots, then the British again and finally the victorious revolutionaries. It wrought hardships on just about everyone along the Ogeechee.

Dublin Plantation was caught up in this maze. The original settler, John Harn, sold the plantation to John Maxwell in 1764. Maxwell was the son of another South Carolina planter who had moved south across the Savannah River. The father, James Maxwell, was a Loyalist, who had served four terms in South Carolina's Royal Assembly, and so was his son. It was John Maxwell who reportedly carved Cherry Hill Plantation out of the ample Dublin Plantation estate.

When the war hit, the Maxwells, like most Americans of the day, did not think the revolution would succeed. After all, the opposition happened to be the most powerful nation on earth and besides, the newness of the Georgia colony meant that most of its people still had very fresh contact with Great Britain. At best, Georgia was a divided colony during the war. It was more a civil war than a revolutionary war along the Ogeechee.

But unlike most Americans, as the war came to a close, John Butler Maxwell did not choose the side of the patriots. He remained loyal to the crown. When the British withdrew, Maxwell remained behind to face the wrath of his patriot neighbors along the Ogeechee. The View from Sterling Bluff was undergirded with strong emotions during those days.

The plantation was officially confiscated by the new State of Georgia in 1782 and part of Cherry Hill Plantation was sold to Captain James Field, sheriff and tax collector of Chatham County. Maxwell was temporarily allowed to remain at Dublin but only "as a prisoner of the sheriff." Maxwell petitioned the state for citizenship and was rejected. He tried to sell part of the property but the state charged him with "embezzlement" as a result. In October of 1784 he was declared to be a fugitive and was reported to be

Savannah today is one of the busiest international seaports on the east coast of the United States.

The shad these 1940's fishermen sought off Sterling Bluff still populate the Ogeechee River.

THE EDISON INSTITUTE, DEARBORN, MICH.

"lurking in some part or place in the state without permission or protection." The order was issued to jail him when captured and transport him to British territory.

This story was played out again and again along the Ogeechee River as the aftermath of war revealed the scars that remained following the conflict. Even so, somehow John Maxwell managed to hold onto Dublin and most of Cherry Hill and was able to later transfer the properties to his daughter.

An Amazing Encounter Along The River

There were numerous military engagements between the British and the patriots on the Ogeechee Neck. For the most part they occurred after the British began retaking Georgia in December of 1778. There are many stories of this phase of local history but perhaps the most fascinating is the tale of what happened at Mr. Savage's Point on the Ogeechee. Thomas Savage, a patriot and native of Bermuda, owned substantial property along the river including his winter home at Silk Hope Plantation (just above Cherry Hill), Sterling Bluff and property near the city of Hardwicke. It was at the latter that a bizarre military engagement took place.

The story involves a British flotilla of four armed vessels, one of 14 guns and three of four guns each. They were manned by 40 seamen with a land force aboard of 111 regular troops, some of them casualties. At their disposal were 130 rifles. The small flotilla was heading down the Ogeechee River seeking to make their way to Savannah when intelligence forces informed them that a revolutionary band was operating along the river downstream.

As a result they decided to anchor for the night and secure their position along the shore with their regular troops. The British were under the command of one Captain French. Into this scene came the creative American patriot Colonel John White, along with six other men:

On the night of October 1, 1779, Colonel John White, Captains George Melvin and A.C.G. Elholm, a sergeant and three privates, seven in all, reconnoitered the position of Captain French, and White determined to capture the party.

The Americans, in pursuance of a well-conceived strategy, built many watch fires around the camp, at such intervals as to lead the British to believe they were surrounded by a large force. During the night, White and his companions marched from fire to fire with the measured tread and the loud challenge of sentinels, hailing from one position and then shifting so rapidly and challenging from the opposite side that the British were completely deceived as to his strength.

The delusion was furthered by having each American mount a horse and ride with haste in various directions, while orders were given in a loud voice.

At the psychological moment, White dashed boldly up to the British camp and demanded a conference with the commander.

Facing Captain French, he said: "I am the commander, sir, of the American soldiers in your vicinity. If you will surrender at once to my force, I will see to it that no injury is done to you or your command. If you decline to do this, I must candidly inform you that the feelings of my troops are highly incensed against you, and I can by no means be responsible for any consequences that may ensue."

Captain French, alarmed over his situation, thanked White for his humanity, and said despondently that it was useless to contend with fate or the large force he saw was around him. He announced his willingness to surrender.

At this moment, Captain Elholm dashed up at full speed, stopped and saluted White. Elholm asked where he should place the artillery.

"Keep them back. Keep them back, sir," White ordered. "The British have surrendered. Move your men off, and send me three guides to conduct them to the American post at Sunbury."

The three guides came forward. The vessels were burned, and the British, anxious to keep out of the way of the enraged and formidable Americans, started for Sunbury at a fast pace, while White remained with the promise he would go to his troops and restrain them. White collected the neighborhood militia, overtook the guides and conducted the party to Sunbury.

The crafty revolutionaries won that encounter but by early 1779, the British were back in control of Georgia. They proceeded to "take into possession all the effects of those who had taken an active part against the King's government" and now the shoe was on the other foot. Governor Wright, who had escaped from young Habersham's house arrest and fled to England, returned when the British retook Savannah.

One of those welcoming the return of the British was Captain James Mackay of Strathy Hall, named after Mackay's ancestral home of Strathnaverin, Scotland. Mackay faithfully served the King under Oglethorpe and was captured with George Washington during the French and Indian War at Great Meadows in 1754.

After the British recaptured Georgia, the Americans made one herculean effort to free Savannah and Georgia from its "captors" and the result was one of the bloodiest defeats for the patriots of the war. In September 1779, a great French Armada with 4,000 troops, many from the West Indies, arrived in support of Benjamin Lincoln's 2,100 troops brought in from South Carolina and local militia. But the Siege of Savannah was for naught.

The well-entrenched British effected a slaughter and the revolutionary strategy henceforth chose to leave coastal Georgia alone, as far as major assaults were concerned. The British ultimately received their mortal wound at Yorktown, Virginia in 1781. In May, 1782, Royal Governor Wright received instructions from London to prepare for the evacuation of Savannah and on July 11, 1782, he delivered the keys of the city to a close friend of Loyalist James Mackay, 25 year old Major James Jackson who settled on the Ogeechee Neck after the war.

3
"YOUR ASSIGNMENT . . . DESTROY THE OGEECHEE BREADBASKET"

Shadows of ancient oaks fall on Strathy Hall Plantation, (right) built long before the American Revolution.

The rice fields of old Richmond Plantation have since become tidal marshes along the Ogeechee.

After the revolution there were scars. This had been not only a revolution that had shaken much of the world but it had obviously impacted those caught up in it on the battlefront as well. There was cruelty and injustice after the war but there were also many examples of remarkable reconciliation.

Healing took place more quickly where there was maturity and some level of respect for the combatant on the other side. Despite the presence of the so-called "Liberty Boys," youths like Colonel James Jackson and the Habersham sons, there was both age and respect for most adversaries along the Ogeechee River. Even the "Liberty Boys" had added seven years to their youth since the advent of the rebellion.

For the most part, the View From Sterling Bluff saw reconciliation get underway rather quickly after the evacuation of the British. Friends of banned Loyalists sought relief for them from the state government, seeking to reverse their losses due to the confiscation and banishment legislation. Slaves were often returned and planters worked together in rebuilding barns and replanting fields that had lain fallow for too long.

Before long most plantations were prosperous once again. There were some new faces on the Neck as military men and more South Carolinians moved in to buy those estates that had been confiscated and put up for sale by the state. The rice yield in Georgia averaged around 10 bushels per acre greater than in South Carolina. That held an obvious attraction for the Carolinians. Soon the rice cultivation had reached new heights and many fortunes were earned or re-earned on the Neck.

The names of the better known plantations have survived to this day – Kilkenny, Belfast, Cottenham, Belvedere, Mount Hope, and of course Silk Hope, Strathy Hall, Sterling Bluff, Cherry Hill and Dublin (Richmond). And there are others, perhaps not as well known but very prominent in their day, such as Egypt, Republican Hall, Cape Genesis Point (Chisholm), Orange Grove, Lincoln, Retreat, Fancy Hall, Star, Milford, Palermo, Ricedale, Waterford, Tiperary, Peacefield, Tranquilla and Tivoli. And an amazing thing about these – Henry Ford would end up owning all of them when he took his turn on the Ogeechee Neck two centuries later.

There were also White Hall, Mulberry Hill, White Oak, Harwood and a few others that would not become Ford's. Across the river there were three more that would, Vallambrosia, Beach Tree and Pine Bluff Plantations.

Changes for Dublin and Cherry Hill
The most prominent estate today, Richmond Hill Plantation, was a relative newcomer as far as the name was concerned. Richmond Plantation would not become Richmond Hill Plantation until Henry Ford called it such but

James Habersham
leased Richmond and
Cherry Hill Planta-
tions after the Revolu-
tionary War.

both were the original Dublin Plantation established by John Harn. The name change came about after John Maxwell's daughter, Mary, had sold Dublin to the Clay family.

Mary ended up with Dublin and Cherry Hill plantations after her Tory father eluded the confiscation legislation of the state of Georgia and deeded the property to her. Perhaps her marriage to patriot hero Lachlan McIntosh of nearby Sunbury had something to do with it.

Some years after her marriage, Mary leased her plantation to Joseph Habersham. This was the same revolutionary who had captured the powder from the magazine in Savannah and sent it to the Patriots at Bunker Hill. Habersham was also mayor of Savannah in 1792, Postmaster General under George Washington and John Adams and an incorporator and director of the Savannah Steamship Company whose ship made the first steam-assisted crossing of the Atlantic in 1819. The Dublin and Cherry Hill leasing to Habersham, probably for rice cultivation, began in 1803 and lasted several years.

In 1820, Mary Maxwell McIntosh sold Dublin to Mary and Thomas Clay, brother and sister, and friends of the Habershams. Their mother was the daughter of Thomas Savage who had owned Silk Hope, Sterling Bluff and the point where the patriot Colonel White had so outwitted English Captain French. The Clays' maternal grandfather, Thomas Savage, Jr., died next door at Silk Hope in 1812. The intertwining of the families along the Ogeechee River became substantial during the two generations after the Revolution.

It apparently was the Clay siblings who changed Dublin's name to Richmond. This was a popular plantation name among the rice plantations of the Carolinas and Georgia, perhaps because of memories of Richmond on the River Thames, in England's Surrey County. Richmond Plantation

An 1834 drawing
shows the slave cabin-
lined oak promenade
to the Cherry Hill
Plantation house.

remained in the Clay family until it was purchased by Henry Weed of Savannah in 1919 who in turn sold it to Henry Ford. The Clays would also end up with Strathy Hall and hold it until the Ford era. They were the largest slave owners on the Neck with 230 owned by 1860.

Cherry Hill Plantation was sold out of the family in 1817 and, after three quick transactions, ended up in the hands of Rhode Island native Richard J. Arnold.

Arnold was engaged in the China trade and remained involved in Providence, Rhode Island where he developed suburban land, wharves and docks. He primarily wintered on the Ogeechee at White Hall Plantation. It was Arnold who brought Rhode Island architecture to the Neck. At Cherry Hill, apparently on the site of the earlier plantation house, he built the Cherry Hill house for his overseer in a style indigenous to the Northern state. The house, though devastated by a tornado (1835), thrice rebuilt and once moved, maintains much of its early distinction to this day.

One of the major planters along the Ogeechee, Arnold also acquired Silk Hope Plantation, Myrtle Grove and the current site of the town of Richmond Hill with Mulberry Hill and Sedgefield Plantation. It was through marriage that he came to own White Hall. Arnold owned 195 slaves and had a reputation for being humane and lenient.

Slaves on rice plantations generally fared better than slaves on cotton or tobacco plantations. Rice plantation slaves usually worked according to a "task" system or a quota basis and their day's work ended whenever the "task" was completed, thus leaving limited time for fishing, relaxing or farming one's own plots. Other slave systems, however, tended to work the laborers from first light to last light.

The slave scene at Cherry Hill was described by a noted American landscape architect, Frederick Law Olmsted, from an 1853 visit to what he called the "show plantations" along the Ogeechee River. In his subsequent book *Seaboard Slave States,* Olmsted describes the slave settlement at Cherry Hill as the area's largest. His descriptions confirm Arnold's reputation as a kind slave owner.

Olmsted was taken with the beauty of the "Richmond-on-Ogeechee House" which Sherman would later burn. He described it as being a two and one-half story frame structure with a piazza extending across the first floor. He described rows of "old live oaks" (now over 135 years old) and said," I have hardly in all my life seen anything so impressively grand and beautiful."

Neck Names

The Ogeechee Neck has had many names in its two and a half centuries of European-rooted dominance. At first it was part of Savannah County as was

The simple palisade at Fort McAllister rebuffed the most violent Yankee naval bombardments.

everything in General Oglethorpe's domain. Next it was part of the Midway District, then the York District, then St. Philip's Parish when Royal Governors began to administer the colony. During the reorganization of the state after the revolution it became part of Liberty County and then on December 19, 1793 Bryan County was carved out of Liberty and Effingham by the Georgia Legislature. It is no wonder that the populace has had its own name for who they are, people of the Ogeechee Neck.

The county's namesake, Jonathan Bryan, was born in South Carolina in 1708, son of an early colonist. He was of "great aid" to General Oglethorpe when he undertook the colonization of Georgia in 1733. Bryan came to Georgia to live in 1752, the year the trustees resigned their charter.

Within three years of his move, he had already become prominent in the colony and was appointed by Governor Reynolds to be Judge of the General Court and later Public Treasurer. Bryan was also a man of faith, a dissenter from the Church of England who subscribed to the Westminster Confession of Faith. He was a friend of John and Charles Wesley and famed English revivalist George Whitefield who impacted the Colonies from Savannah to Boston and founded the nearby Bethesda Orphanage in Georgia, now considered the oldest in America.

Bryan planted a church, "a meeting house," in Savannah and an old faithful servant of his named Andrew founded the first black church in America there. "His heart was full of kindness," reads an old record. "To his neighbors he was obliging, to his servants remarkably indulgent; and to his praise be it said, that he took active measures to supply them with the ministrations of the Gospel."

Bryan was also a friend of liberty and clearly sided with the patriots, causing the Governor to call for his resignation from royal offices and responsibilities. This he did at age 66 but that was not enough for the British who dispatched a man-of-war and a party of armed men to take him and his son prisoner.

Ways Station

Another name that would come to the Ogeechee Neck and then pass away during the Ford era was Ways Station. The reason for the name had to do with the coming of a new age to the Neck, the railroad age. An expanded world would come on the railroad. War would come on it and Henry Ford would come on it as well.

The year was 1856 and the first line to come through Bryan County was the Atlantic Coast Line. It was a great day since up to that time the best avenue of transport was up and down the river. There were the dirt paths for ox carts, mules and horses but those were usually inefficient, muddy or dusty. It was the river that was frequented with sail-powered craft hauling

supplies to and from Savannah for the plantations. Rice was exported that way as was the increasingly sizable cotton crop.

The railroad usually called each of its new stations by the name of a prominent citizen. Thus when the time came to name the new station on the Ogeechee Neck, the usual search was made. Apparently the most prominent person in the neighborhood at the time was William J. Way.

That same year Way had been appointed Postmaster of the new post office built at what is now Richmond Hill. So when the railroad came through the area, its stop was called "Ways" or "Ways Station."

Another name that would play an important part in the history of the area was McAllister. George W. McAllister bought Strathy Hall from Captain Mackay's estate on May 6, 1817. McAllisters have been Georgia attorney generals, senators, mayors of Savannah and held places of prominence from New York City to California. A McAllister daughter would also become the wife of one of the Clays of Richmond Plantation.

George W. McAllister also owned Genesis Point, a commanding shoreline bluff on the Ogeechee River below Hardwicke and Savage's Point. When McAllister died, he left Genesis Point as well as Strathy Hall to his son, Joseph L. McAllister who organized the Hardwicke Mounted Riflemen. During the Civil War, the mounted Riflemen would become Company H of the 7th Georgia Cavalry. McAllister was killed in action in 1864 while his regiment was under Jeb Stuart's command.

Fort McAllister

One of the most successful forts the Confederate Army would ever build was constructed on Genesis Point. It is debated to this day which of the McAllisters it was named for but about its remarkable service there is no debate. For the vast majority of the conflict, Fort McAllister would again and again keep the Northern forces from getting into the heartland of the Ogeechee Neck. Getting access to the Neck was one of the things the Union Army wanted most because they had their own name for it – "The Ogeechee Breadbasket."

When the war started to take shape, the vital role of the Neck became clear in a hurry. It was one of the few food raising locations in the South that was well defended. During the war a vast amount of grain was produced for the Confederate troops there.

Frederick Olmsted's 1853 description of either the Cherry Hill or Richmond-on-Ogeechee agricultural operations illustrates the validity of the Union's concerns. From the slave settlement at Cherry Hill, Olmsted reported driving to a rice mill which he described as:

A monster barn with more and better machinery for threshing and storing of rice, driven by a steam engine, than I have ever seen used for grain on any farm in Europe or America before.

Olmsted also described shops and sheds with slaves working as blacksmiths, carpenters and mechanics. He described tool rooms, corn rooms, mule stables, pig lots, storerooms and large gardens in addition to the rice Gelds. An 1860 Rhode Island insurance policy taken out by Richard Arnold on Cherry Hill also mentions a thrashing machine and elevator buildings, a brick engine house, sugar house, steam engine and boiler building, grist mill and stables.

The Southern coast was blockaded by Union ships, cutting off any international trade, but the internal supply lines via the new railroad were kept intact for most of the war. In 1861, Fort McAllister was constructed at Genesis Point to protect the "breadbasket" and to provide the southernmost link in the chain of Confederate defenses surrounding Savannah.

In November 1861, Robert E. Lee was the Commander of the Military Department of the Coasts of South Carolina, Georgia and East Florida. His headquarters were at a railroad junction in Coosawhatchie, South Carolina, an old Indian village and the place where he purchased his famous horse "Traveler." From that location Lee could move efficiently by rail among his posts and manage his departmental command.

The famed general made at least one inspection tour of Fort McAllister before his elevation to the command of the Army of Northern Virginia. A

Relics of lettuce barns from the first quarter of this century still stand along the river.

statue of the famed general on his horse Traveler now stands alongside the ancient road he traveled through Cherry Hill Plantation on the way to the fort.

Attacks on Fort McAllister

Fort McAllister was not one of the most beautiful forts in the Confederacy. It did not have impressive brick walls like those at nearby Fort Pulaski guarding the mouth of the Savannah River. From a budget for defense standpoint, its modest appearance seemed like a poor economy considering the importance of the terrain it was defending. It was simply a crude fortress with palisades of spiked logs around a moat configuration and walls that in essence were mounds of sandy earth. Yet it was precisely the right concept.

The sandy banks of the fort were blasted again and again by federal gunboats only to settle back in place so that at night only a little work would make the ramparts as good as new. Finally the federal assault ships would conclude that they were wasting their ammunition and should leave the fort alone until it could be attacked in a different manner.

In July and November of 1862, Union warships launched the first attacks on the fort but inflicted little damage. The Emmet Rifles and the Republican Blues defending the fort on those occasions received only three men wounded.

On January 27, 1863, the stakes were raised as the Union threw the ironclad "Montauk" against the fort. Above the fort lay a taunting nemesis to the Yankee fleet, the exceedingly swift Confederate blockade runner "Nashville," awaiting an opportunity to exit the Ogeechee. Containing a cargo of resin, cotton and tobacco, the ship had escaped capture in Charleston and taken refuge behind the guns of Fort McAllister.

The "Montauk" steamed up to the obstructions put in the river below the fort by the rebels, followed by the gunboats "Seneca," "Wissahichen," "Dawn" and "Williams" which anchored a mile astern. The battle was engaged and raged for four hours with exceedingly accurate fire coming from Fort McAllister, the ironclad being repeatedly hit but to no consequence because of the armor. The fire of the federals was ineffective and the flotilla withdrew once their ammunition was exhausted.

A fiercer engagement was fought on February 1. Prior to that engagement, the guns from the blockade runner, renamed the CSS Rattlesnake, were removed and installed in a battery on a bluff next to Richmond Plantation as back up protection for the vital railroad bridge near Ways Station.

In this engagement, the "Montauk" was hit 46 times by the accurate guns of McAllister but the weight of the shot was not sufficient to do the ironclad any harm. This was one of the federal's best offensives against the

A Yankee fleet attacks Fort McAllister while the ironclad Montauk sinks the CSS Rattlesnake.

sandy fortress, according to the fort's Colonel Anderson:

> At times their fire was terrible. Their mortar firing was usually fine, a large number of their shells bursting directly over the battery. The ironclad's fire was principally directed at the 8 inch Columbiad, and about 8:15 o'clock the parapet in front of this gun was so badly breached as to leave the gun entirely exposed. The detachment did not leave their gun or evince the slightest fear but in a most gallant and determined manner fought their gun to the close of the action, refusing to be relieved.

The "Montauk" finally withdrew having wounded seven soldiers, killing the fort's commander and disabling a 32-pounder. Four weeks later, on February 27, the blockade runner was testing the waters near the fort and ran aground not far from the Confederate obstructions in the river. The following day the "Montauk" steamed to within range of the ship, determined to finish her off.

It was a violent scene with the fortress desperately bombarding the ironclad while its sister ships rained fire on the fort. Before long the "Nashville" was in flames from the "Montauk's" accurate fire. Immediately the northern press widely heralded the demise of the elusive rebel ship with artists' depictions of the scene appearing in papers around the world.

On March 3, 1863, the Union threw three monitors into the assault against Fort McAllister and fired on the fort for seven hours during the day and all night. The only effect was to temporarily dismount the 8-inch gun and the 42-pounder plus wound two men slightly. The fort was as good as ever the next morning. This led Admiral Dupont, who was preparing to attack Charleston, to report: "Whatever degree of impenetrability the monitor might have, there was no corresponding quality destructiveness against the fort."

Horace Greeley, in his "American Conflict," said that from this time the Union fleets "saved" their ammunition by letting Fort McAllister alone. It would be another year and a half before Fort McAllister would be attacked again.

The Fall and the Aftermath

With the failure of the naval strategy, infantryman General William Tecumseh Sherman was given orders to destroy the Ogeechee breadbasket from the other direction. This he effectively did. In his infamous "March to the Sea" he either carried off all the food stores on the Ogeechee Neck or destroyed them. All the rice mills were burned in late 1864 as were most of the plantation homes, such as Silk Hope, Cherry Hill, Richmond Plantation and scores of others. Sherman's forces wrote home about the grand lifestyle in which they lived during their time of destruction along the Ogeechee.

They delighted in replacing their rations of hard tack with sweet potatoes and dining on fresh beef and pork instead of their usual salt pork.

On December 13, 1864 the massive land force came to a tantalizing objective, Fort McAllister. The fort was not really designed to withstand a substantial land assault and Sherman expected no difficulty. A Major Kilpatrick was charged with taking the fort with the regiment under his command. Local legend has it that Sherman and Kilpatrick conferred before the assault, possibly at Kilkenny Plantation.

Kilpatrick was no newcomer to the Ogeechee Neck having spent a summer at Lebanon Plantation with the brother of Major George Anderson, Jr., by then the defending commander of Fort McAllister. Kilpatrick selected the familiar Lebanon Plantation as his assault headquarters. The story says that Kilpatrick told General Sherman in their conference that he did not think his one regiment could take the fort. Sherman is reported to have expressed profane disdain at the assessment telling his major that there were only 250 men in the garrison.

Kilpatrick is reported to have replied, "Yes, the garrison is not large, but I know the man commanding, and he is fool enough not to surrender." The fort was finally carried in 15 minutes when nine regiments of 4,500 men swarmed over it. Indeed, Major Anderson did not surrender it. General Sherman was watching the assault from atop a rice mill on the other side of the Ogeechee at Vallambrosia Plantation.

In the assault the federals lost four officers killed, seven commissioned officers and 103 men wounded. The Confederates lost 12 men killed, 21 wounded and 195 taken prisoner along with 60 tons of ammunition.

The emotional moment of the fort's capitulation is captured in the report of the event sent to the Union General in charge of the military division of the Mississippi by an aide-de-camp, "Dear General: Take a good big drink, a long breath, and then yell like the devil. The fort was carried at 4:30 p.m."

Local lore also has passed down an after-the-battle tale. In the confusing aftermath of the assault, the Confederate prisoners reportedly were confined in the corral of the Union's Lebanon Plantation headquarters, the home of the fort's Commander, Major Anderson.

In a severe breach of protocol (if true), Major Anderson was there incarcerated with his men. The story goes on to report that Major Kilpatrick, seeking his old friend, found him there, wounded, tired and disgusted, Anderson having been knocked in the head with a musket.

"This is all the scoundrels left of me," Anderson complained to Kilpatrick. "It's adding insult to injury to coop me up in my own pig pen."

Old Dublin Plantation, later to be Richmond Plantation, as it exists today.

The original antebellum Cherry Hill Plantation house has been rebuilt several times over the years.

"Don't worry about that," Kilpatrick said. "Go clean up and you can sleep in your own bed."

General Sherman continued on to Savannah and within a short time had encircled the city on all sides but one, by which the Confederate defenders retreated. The city was surrendered to Sherman by civilian officials who pleaded for the invaders to spare the city. This Sherman did, wiring President Lincoln that he had completed his march to the sea, and was giving him Savannah, spared from destruction, as a Christmas present.

After the war, the thing that had driven many Southerners to arms and justified in their own minds the rightness of their cause, happened – the economy absolutely collapsed, particularly on the Ogeechee Neck. There was no justifying an institution such as slavery but the Southern planters were right in that the loss of it would ruin them and their part of the country.

Had Oglethorpe and the trustees persisted in their initial ban of slavery, Georgians, at least, would not have had the opportunity to paint themselves into such a financial and ethical corner. But that did not happen.

Literally overnight, the View From Sterling Bluff changed from looking out on one of the most prosperous landscapes in the nation to one of the poorest. The booming rice economy crashed as suddenly as the fall of Fort McAllister. The dire essential of the rice industry was cheap labor and without slaves, there was none. Rice planting continued on a one-third scale until a devastating hurricane in 1887 destroyed dikes, crops and equipment. Cotton cultivation continued on a small scale and then the boll weevil came and took that. A cotton gin was still standing at Richmond Plantation when Henry Ford came to the country.

Most of the planters moved away and most of the plantations fell into complete disrepair. Unlike the days after the Revolutionary War, there was little fixing things up and replanting. Former slaves remained and scratched out a living but many of them were ill-equipped for the responsibilities thrust upon them. These were very difficult times. By the early years of the twentieth century, Bryan County consisted of small, poor farms, poor-paying sawmills, some turpentine production, some outsider-owned hunt clubs, a large degree of subsistence living from the fish and oysters of the river and a lot of moonshining. Disease from intestinal parasites such as hook worm plus malaria was rampant. The darkest days in its modern history had quickly descended upon the people who lived along the Ogeechee River. It was into this scene that a stranger from Michigan would unexpectedly step. He would come a stranger but Henry Ford would leave a friend.

4
HENRY FORD COMES
TO GEORGIA

Henry Ford was the world's first billionaire and unrivaled king of the new industrial age.

At first glance, even after many long looks, Ways Station, Georgia, seems like the last place on earth that a billionaire like Henry Ford might want to settle, even for a few months a year. Think of it. Here was a man who could have built a personal retreat anywhere on the face of the earth and he chose Ways Station! Just one look at Ways Station in the mid-twenties would bring absolute perplexity to any thinking individual.

At the time, fifteen years before Ways Station would become Richmond Hill, the little crossroads was characterized by an abundance of moonshine stills, a poor saw mill, rampant unemployment and raging malaria. They did have some interesting history, a beautiful river and a whistle stop on the railroad track. But one would hardly even think that a man of Henry Ford's stature would give the place a second thought.

What is more, in 1923, Henry Ford was considered a prime candidate for the Presidency of the United States. Without his cooperation, he had been entered in several state primary elections in 1916 and had fared extremely well, winning Michigan and coming in second in California and Nebraska. Now he was leading in the 1923 Presidential polls.

Then too, the Ford Motor Company was considered the greatest industrial enterprise in the entire world with profits since its inception at around $1 billion. The Ford enterprise owned 31 assembly plants, mines and vast timber lands. Total Ford employment, direct and indirect, was estimated to exceed 500,000 men. Ford railroads transported Ford coal and iron ore from Ford mines and Ford freighters brought in rubber from overseas. Ford manufactured aircraft, like the Ford Tri-motor, ferried Ford executives to and from various Ford ventures such as the thousands of acres of Ford pine forests.

And he came to Ways Station?

The reasons why can begin to be pieced together from some of the other things that were going on in 1923 and those middle years of the twenties. For one thing, Ford friend Harvey Firestone was upset about the British corner on the world's rubber market.

Rubber, Education and a Naturalist

The British were arbitrarily doubling the world's rubber price and Firestone, who had a burgeoning tire business, was upset. The result of a conversation with his friend Henry, antagonist of the British, would be a research project to find a native American source of rubber and break the British monopoly. The ambitious project would include not only Firestone and Ford but also an old boss of Ford, Thomas Edison. In 1924, the three men would organize the Edison Botanic Research Corporation and begin their search for Ameri-

Ford's Richmond Hill mansion was built on the site of the Sherman-burned Dublin Plantation.

Henry Ford personally inspects a poor Bryan County homestead. He often provided assistance to such neighbors.

L-R, Ford is shown with Thomas Edison and Harvey Firestone, partners in the Edison Botanic Institute.

THE EDISON INSTITUTE, DEARBORN, MICH.

THE EDISON INSTITUTE, DEARBORN, MICH.

Planted by John Harn around 1747, massive oaks (right) still stand at Sterling Bluff Plantation.

can rubber on some acreage they purchased in Fort Myers, Florida. The work would end up on the shores of the Ogeechee River.

Another significant thing happened in 1923. Henry and wife Clara Ford paid a visit to Rome, Georgia on returning from a Southern vacation trip. The object of their visit was an unusual school founded by Martha Berry, daughter of a wealthy Rome family who was raised in a classic antebellum Georgia mansion. Miss Berry grew up in elegance but behind the mansion in the mountains dwelt semi-literate whites struggling for survival in their Appalachian log cabins.

Burdened by their plight, Miss Berry opened the Berry School in 1902 to train the "Cracker" boys in farm and industrial skills. It was a highly practical ministry which greatly appealed to both the pragmatist and the supporter of the underdog in Henry Ford. When the Fords visited the school in 1923 there were 600 students, 3,000 graduates, a prosperous farming and animal husbandry program and a Ford tractor working the fields. Everybody worked, the boys in the fields and the girls with practical crafts of the farmer's wife and just about everybody earned his way through the school.

At the time, Ford had a number of schools he was supporting in Massachusetts, Michigan and England, along the same lines as Miss Berry's but less comprehensive. He was enamored with the work at Rome and during the 1920's generously poured almost $4 million into the school. His vision for this kind of innovative educational approach had been enlarged. He would soon transfer his refreshed educational zeal to the little Ways Station community on the Ogeechee River.

Another factor determining Ford's interest in coastal Georgia involved John Burroughs, dean of American naturalists of Ford's day and personal friend of the auto magnate.

John Burroughs generally is given credit for Henry Ford coming to Ways Station. One prominent story is that the naturalist, Ford, Firestone and Edison were on the way to Florida for a vacation outing in 1925 and as their train crossed the Ogeechee River, Burroughs pointed down the river and said, "Good bird watching country." The story has one major flaw. Burroughs died in 1921.

Another story has the group touring the Georgia coast by boat in 1915 with Burrough's making the same statement as they passed the mouth of the Ogeechee River. R.L. Cooper, the Savannah real estate agent who handled the Ogeechee Neck acquisitions for Ford, relates that, according to Ford himself, Burroughs indeed had suggested Georgia to the Fords because it "had a better climate and was a better place in winter than Florida."

One local Richmond Hill tale has Henry returning north from Florida in his chauffeured limousine and, out of curiosity, turning off Route 17 down what is now "Ford Highway." There he was struck by the extreme needs of the people, particularly the children. His response – involvement, medical help, schools and jobs. This version could fit with other insights.

Cooper's 1951 oral history in the Ford archives in Dearborn, Michigan, tells of Ford's personal secretary in Michigan, Frank Campsall, coming in the office in December 1925 and introducing himself as Mr. Carroll of Chicago and desiring to "look over some country properties." The real estate agent took "Mr. Carroll" from Brunswick, Georgia to Charleston, South Carolina, showing him large plantation properties. Ironically, they traveled in Mr. Cooper's Model T Ford.

"The second day he came in and reintroduced himself as Mr. Campsall," recalled Cooper, "secretary to Henry Ford. This knocked me off my feet! He (Mr. Campsall) said Mr. Ford was in town and desired to look over the Bryan County property." Later that day, the Fords, Campsall and Cooper toured Richmond Plantation, Cherry Hill and Strathy Hall with the Fords making their decision to buy. "Purchase all of the lands along the Ogeechee River east of the Coastal Highway (Route 17)," Ford told Cooper.

Cooper gave Ford some real estate patter about the money which could be made off the property, only to be cut short by the automaker who said that, "he was not interested in making money, that he had made more money from motor cars than he could spend." Ford "hinted," to use Cooper's word, "that he was much interested in the Martha Berry School at Mt. Berry in upper Georgia."

For whatever immediate reason, in 1925, Henry Ford started purchasing land in the Sterling Bluff area, with the three historic plantations the group visited. By the time he was finished, Ford Farms or Richmond Hill Plantation as he would call his mansion house, would total around 70,000 acres and cover over 120 square miles. That amounts to a principality stretching more than 30 miles on both sides of the Ogeechee River with Ways Station roughly in the middle. Included were villages, islands, marshes, plantations, timber and schools.

Richmond Hill also was to be a vehicle of withdrawal for Henry. It would not have been for other people because of all the special problems of the place at that time. But for Henry, it was perfect. These problems were his recreation. It brought together a host of the elements that gave satisfaction and meaning to Ford while providing him escape from those things that distressed him.

5
THE ENORMOUS CHALLENGE

Henry Ford built the "Trade School" at Ways Station to train unemployed residents and students.

THE EDISON INSTITUTE, DEARBORN, MICH.

The history of what happened along the Ogeechee River appears to be a massive social experiment. And to a degree it was. Henry Ford had some very definite ideas of how men were motivated, what was really helpful to them and what was true education. "Helping people is my religion," he would later tell a local laborer. He understood a great deal about the heartbeat of these country people and most of his plans for them were very good.

The ways in which Ford would help the people of the Ogeechee Neck were varied. He was foundational in his approach to things so before some of his grander ideas could be tried, he knew there were some basic problems to overcome.

The Malaria Challenge
While the Ford men were assembling the massive acreage that would become Ford's Georgia fiefdom during the late 1920's and early 30's, a medical team from Dearborn was doing some assembling of its own. It was conducting a health inventory of the area. The results were shocking. Over half of the residents of the Ford portion of Bryan County had malaria and a similarly large percentage were infected with hookworm. There also were

typhoid, smallpox and diphtheria. Upon learning these facts, Henry simply told his staff to do whatever was necessary to eliminate that condition.

Mosquitoes and malarial fever are well known partners in crime. The battle against both in Ways Station typically had been fought with a combination of "flit" guns for the mosquitoes and quinine for the fever they carried. But Henry Ford brought a better way, a massive program that ranged from an extensive county-wide drainage program to eliminate breeding areas to the latest medical tactics. The goal was nothing less than to make Ways Station and Bryan County one of the most desirable places to live in the entire South.

To attack the medical problem along the Ogeechee, Henry dispatched several doctors, nurses and some drainage specialists to Georgia to do the job. The districts in which Ford holdings lay were mapped out and each home was indicated on the map. Each of the nurses was assigned to specific homes and put in charge of overseeing the eradication of the diseases found there. The massive assault was coordinated out of two medical clinics built by Ford in 1931.

People came to Ford-built clinics from 25 miles "back in the woods," after walking or riding carts over muddy roads. The nurses visited their

The Ogeechee River bends away from the old Richmond Plantation rice fields.

The Ford-built Martha-Mary Chapel (right) today is the Roman Catholic Church in Richmond Hill.

Students and their teacher pose in front of a rural school later replaced by Henry Ford.

THE EDISON INSTITUTE, DEARBORN, MICH.

assigned homes twice daily. Bulldozers were everywhere draining swamps in Bryan County. It was an all-fronts attack on malaria or "Black Water Fever" as it was called locally.

Within one year, new cases of malaria dropped by 99% and the presence of hookworm parasites showed a parallel decline. Educational programs on hygiene, diet and the provision of free plumbing facilities further terminated the days when malaria and parasites were an accepted part of life in the area.

Educational Assault

Spurred on by his experience in Rome, Ford also focused on education along the Ogeechee. The education picture in Bryan County, as in much of the deep South, had been complicated by the health situation and the economy. Poor soil has always produced poor folks and the destructive health cycle of the area merely amplified that misery.

But with the health picture dramatically altered, Ford set out to attack the educational deprivation on the Ogeechee Neck. In the early thirties, when the resources of the Ford team were first turned to education, the then-segregated schooling program in the county consisted of a small school house for white children and six buildings described as "abandoned woodsheds" for blacks scattered throughout the more rural parts of the district.

Within time, all the black school sites were purchased by Ford as part of the extensive land acquisition program. These hopelessly inadequate "school shacks" were open only five months a year and experienced very low attendance. Henry Ford quickly moved to provide some stop-gap measures to improve the situation.

The buildings were improved, educational equipment such as McGuffey Readers, libraries, movie projectors, radios and athletic uniforms were put in the hands of the faculty and the teachers themselves were directly paid for an additional four months of service so the schools could operate for a full nine-month term. Later the local school board would gradually extend the months of teachers' salaries but Henry would always provide for the missing months.

Ford also undertook the enlarging of the white school including the addition of a lunch room. Free hot lunches, planned along Ford's ever present nutrition emphasis, were provided to all the students. He also supplied the students with free medical and dental care at the two health clinics built to combat malaria and parasites and even set up a school bus transportation system with Ford vehicles.

For further training of the boys a trade school was established. In this

school the boys were taught metal working, woodwork, the printer's art and other such skills. The students reached such a level of accomplishment that the print shop met all the needs of Ford's local operations and the wood shop did the same with furniture as well as selling large quantities to nearby military bases. Metal and iron work also spilled over into the general public's consumption.

Henry had a strong affinity for the local children from the outset. According to a 1951 oral history of Tom Phillips, lifetime resident of the community and manager of the sawmill, there would be a state of hyperactivity among the children whenever Mr. Ford would come to town. He would give parties for the youngsters and spend time with them from the kindergarten level to the oldest.

> When it was time for Mr. Ford to arrive, every child would dress up in his best clothes and watch that railroad track. They'd come home from school and if they had a sad look on their faces, we'd know the train hadn't come in. If they were all smiles, we knew Mr. Ford was here. He really loved youth ... the children just worshipped him.

The Spirit of George Washington Carver

When Henry Ford decided the time had come to do away with the upgraded "woodshed schools" for blacks and provide them a modern consolidated school, he looked to an old friend to provide a spark to the vision. George Washington Carver, at the time professor at Tuskegee Institute in Alabama, was a famous person among the black residents of the South.

Carver was a highly skilled botanist who discovered 300 uses for the peanut and 188 products in the sweet potato. He was one of the few nationally known personalities to ever be invited to Ford's estate in Georgia. He also visited Dearborn where the press delighted in reporting stories of Carver and the auto magnate eating dandelion and grass sandwiches for lunch.

The new school that Henry Ford would build for the black children would bear the famed scientist's name. It would be a modern grammar and high school and have a lunch room, a dormitory for teachers, a machine shop and its own school buses.

Another feature of the George Washington Carver School was adult education. There were courses in sewing, handicraft, and manual arts for men. But the course that attracted most of the old people was the reading class, which also featured writing and math. The key to the popularity was revealed when the teacher wisely asked what textbook his students would like to study. The following account was from an eye witness:

> With one accord, but with the confusion of Babel, adults expressed their

Mr. and Mrs. Ford stand with George Washington Carver in front of Ford's new consolidated school.

the answers – "The Blessed Word" – "The Good Book" – "Scriptures" – So by their own choice the Bible became their reading text. The choice must have been guided by Providence, because no other printed word, no matter how expertly compiled, could have held their attention through the trying hours of separating one word from another.

The adult program brought a lot of satisfaction to teacher and pupil alike. To encourage the night school work, Henry Ford made it a rule that all of his employees should sign their names for their pay checks instead of "making their mark," as was often the custom. After many months of night classes, one Richard Davis, aged 65, finally succeeded in making the change from "mark" to signature, albeit larger than the space provided. When asked his reaction to the big day, the Ford employee responded as follows:

> I just took mah pay and said, "thanky, suh" but in mah heart I'se signin' and prayin' and I'se feelin' good all ovah. I suah is delighted, yassah, an' I keeps on tryin' to write smaller and smaller.

The George Washington Carver School was opened in 1939 with six teachers and 198 students. By the time of a newspaper article on the school four years later, it had grown to 300 children and 12 teachers. In addition there was a farm of 100 acres with 400 red hens, two kinds of hogs, two Ford tractors, one mule and a wagon to take the produce the children raised to market. The Henry Ford brand of education was very practical indeed.

Tom Phillips worked for Henry Ford at Ways Station and he, like so many others in the community-tended to look back on his community in terms of "before and after" the arrival of Henry Ford:

> Before Ford came, there wasn't anything here. People was awful poor. When they got work they had to go off and get it, white and colored alike. Indeed, this was a poor place before Ford came here.

Not everybody would have agreed with the extreme way that Tom Phillips made the point but there was no denying that the man from Michigan had a profound impact on the sleepy little community. The impact came not only from the wonderful things that were done in the school system and the new roads he "pushed in" here and there or even the great deliverance he provided from malaria and hookworms. "Mister Ford" also brought about a great social impact on the town as well.

The Community House
One of the most intriguing projects in this regard was the "Community House." Built around 1937, the 18-room house held a dominant place structurally and socially in Ways. Its primary function was to expand the practical horizons of the local school girls who were formed into groups that took turns living in the house one week at a time.

The Community House was described as providing instruction in the "home arts." A resident "hostess" and home economics teacher utilized spacious kitchens and other operations of the house to provide useful orientation to "serving, cooking, housekeeping and other phases of domestic science."

"We planned all the meals, did all the shopping, cooking, serving and clean up," recalled Margaret Fennell, former student and the secretary in the Ford office in Ways from 1944 to 1951. "There was canning and sewing as well. Each class of girls spent a week there every six weeks or so. For us, it was like going to Heaven!"

The unusual educational facility also contained a large ballroom, reportedly inspired and copied from a ballroom in the Cottenham Plantation house, which supplied most of the timber and main mantlepiece for the Community House. Old-fashioned dancing, particularly square dancing, was avidly promoted by Henry Ford all over the country. He loathed the dancing innovations of the 1920's, the "black bottom" and the "Charleston" and sought to strengthen the influence of dances which "have lasted through the years," including waltzes. One of Ford's attachments to the South reportedly was its heritage of generating music appropriate to the Ford taste as well as "folk dancing."

Dancing lessons were a regular part of the children's curriculum at the Community Center and public dances were a frequent event. The quadrille, a slower square dance, was particularly emphasized. Groups from Savannah and other counties often were invited to participate. Mr. and Mrs. Ford frequently attended themselves and took part enthusiastically. On one occasion, according to a former office manager, Mrs. Ford berated her husband for dancing excessively at his age. "Now, Henry, you've danced enough!" she is reported to have said. "Sit down now, Henry. You've got to rest."

Town Chapels
Next door to the Community Center, Henry Ford built one of two chapels he gave to the people of Ways. Having some rather unconventional religious beliefs personally, the auto magnate nonetheless felt that the churchless village of Ways ought to have a church as part of the community's backbone. So he built two chapels, one for the black community and one for the white.

It was next to the Community House that Ford built the Martha-Mary Chapel, a white spired, New England styled building patterned after the chapel by the same name he built in Greenfield Village. The name comes from the first names of the mothers of Henry and Clara Ford.

6
RICHMOND HILL PLANTATION

Henry Ford built a tunnel connecting the mansion to the old rice mill and power generator.

It was in 1935 that the Fords made a definite decision to build a residence in Georgia. They selected the site of the old Richmond Plantation, which had been burned by Sherman on his "march to the sea." The site was on a high bluff overlooking the Great Ogeechee River, about ten stones' throws from Sterling Bluff.

Clara Ford took the helm in planning the Southern retreat. She had long envisioned a dream house with columns, wide verandas, magnificent staircases and large spacious rooms. The Ford refurbished Cherry Hill Plantation house, about two miles up the river, was not spacious enough nor columned as Mrs. Ford desired. The Cherry Hill House did have a picturesque river side porch, provided marvelous vistas and was approached by a classic live oak promenade but it was just not what she had in mind. A new house, a Southern mansion, would have to be built.

Old Savannah provided a host of inspirations for such an undertaking. One ideal inspiration settled on by the Fords was the Hermitage Plantation, on the Savannah River, just upstream from Savannah. It was built in the 1820's by Henry McAlpin, a native Scot who had established a brick plant nearby that produced what is known today as "Savannah grey" bricks, a soft hued, rouge-colored brick that is as "Savannah" as the picturesque town squares. There McAlpin had built a beautiful Greek Revival style mansion with his bricks plus marble steps.

It had been one of the showplaces of the area for years, even after the roof caved in. Some of General Sherman's men had been quartered there and the famous silent film director Francis X. Bushman had filmed "Under Silent Skies" there.

It was not precisely what the Fords had in mind but it was very close. Envisioned was a two story portico with continuous columns spanning both stories over the entrance. The Hermitage had that look but lacked the sweep of a full two story elevation. Yet in 1935, the Fords purchased the Hermitage for $10,000 to demolish it for those beautiful bricks and rebuild a Ford expanded version of the old house on Richmond Plantation, or Richmond Hill as he came to call the high bluff with its dramatic vista overlooking the river. "Anything not a swamp around here is named a hill," Ford once told a local reporter. John Harn had first called it Dublin Plantation in 1747.

The dismantling of the old Hermitage was not entirely a popular idea in Savannah. An historical preservation group was created to save the old plantation, this being years before such organizations became vogue. Headed by Secretary of Interior Harold Ickes, the group failed in its efforts with Henry promising to create an even better southern mansion of classical Greek Revival influence along the Ogeechee. He hired prominent Savannah architect Cletus W. Bergen to do the job.

The original Richmond Hill Plantation house (left) was built by Henry Ford for his wife Clara in 1938.

Sterling Creek passes to the right of the now-flooded Richmond Hill rice fields.

Clara and Henry Ford
break ground for
Clara's "Dream House"
in 1936.

The new version of the Hermitage actually would not only reflect the Greek Revival Period but also Federal and Georgian architecture. This diversity kept the house from simply being an elevated reproduction of the Hermitage which, while displeasing to some, was appropriate for a man like Henry Ford who copied no man.

Clara Ford devoted months to meticulously planning the house, even having a 1/12 scale model of the house created for these purposes. The house had a removable wooden roof to accommodate the scale-model wooden furnishings she also ordered. The model is on display today in the Dearborn Museum.

A Grand House

Clara and Henry personally broke ground for their newest and most beautiful home in 1936. It was completed in 1938 with its colossal portico and sweeping "Temple in the Winds" columns on both the front and river sides of the house.

The front door faced the south with a Federal influence and leaded glass fanlight. Central halls ran front to rear on both floors and the first floor featured a full depth ballroom. A favorite room for the Fords was the library with a beautiful fireplace. Mrs. Ford got her magnificent staircase which led to six bedrooms and seven baths on the second floor. Mr. Ford's bedroom had two bathrooms.

The grand house had everything the old South did not have including air conditioning and an elevator. Most of the furnishings came out of the museum in Dearborn but still seemed comfortably plain. The living room was overhung by magnificent chandeliers. One chandelier cost $65,000 and only one person, Ford's master mechanic in Dearborn, was allowed to dust it. In the massive kitchen and pantry, Mrs. Ford stored $150,000 worth of crystal and china.

Outside, some of the largest live oaks in Georgia provided an almost fictional setting for 55 acres of manicured lawn and flowering gardens planned to bloom during the Fords' traditional early spring months in residence. Camellias, azaleas, tea olives, dogwoods, quinces and Japanese magnolias were planned to provide a pink and white perfumed wonderland for the Michigan couple.

Wildlife abounded on the property and Ford's ever present birdhouses were tucked in the appropriate places. Ford forbade hunting on the property and before long deer and wild hogs began to abound and even wild turkeys became tame and frequented the lawn during the day.

One year, Clara Ford proposed having one of the watchmen go out and snatch up a turkey for a special dinner. "No, Sir," Henry was reported to have bellowed. "You send to town for a turkey if you want one!"

The Ford-protected deer grew to such numbers that they became a problem with both flowers and crops. One farm superintendent, when instructed to plant soybeans on the old Silk Hope Plantation, commented that the deer were a major problem over there. "Well," said Mr. Ford, "just plant enough for the deer and for us."

Landscapers at the Fords' home were hard pressed to stay ahead of the deer, too. "They loved violets as much as Mrs. Ford did." The solution was to make morning inspections of the violet beds and rush off to the greenhouse for replacements if the deer had been through the night before.

Shortly after the Richmond Hill house was completed, and the Fords were in residence, Henry expressed the wish that the entire 70,000 acres of Ford Farms be called Richmond Hill Plantation and that perhaps the name of the town and post office might also be thus altered. The matter was taken in hand by J.F. Gregory, Ford's local General Manager, who was described as "a hard-fisted, gun toting, native Georgian." Even today he is recalled with mixed reviews by the people who worked for him.

The officials of the two railroads with tracks running through the town readily agreed to the change but the post office advised Gregory that a public petition would be required to effect such a change. When the local population heard about Mr. Ford's desire, over 700 rushed to sign the petition as a personal favor to the man who had done so much for the community. On May 1, 1941 the name of Ways Station was changed to Richmond Hill by order of the department and amidst great ceremony in the town.

Feral pigs still run
wild in Sterling Bluff
Plantation.

The remains of the Richmond rice mill, destroyed by General Sherman shown as Henry Ford found it.

THE EDISON INSTITUTE, DEARBORN, MICH.

Ford restored the mill and converted it to a power station and personal laboratory.

THE EDISON INSTITUTE, DEARBORN, MICH.

The Tunnel and Tinkering

"Everywhere that Mary went the lamb was sure to go" goes the nursery rhyme. A similar verse could be coined about Henry Ford with steam plants and tunnels taking the place of the lamb. In just about every venture where construction was involved, Henry had to include a tunnel in it and one that usually connected to a steam plant. This was the case at Richmond Hill as well.

Downstairs from the Richmond Hill mansion's kitchen is an inconspicuous looking door. It leads to "the tunnel." The tunnel, with the steam pipes that are also a kind of Ford trademark, runs parallel to the avenue of oaks to the east of the plantation house, under the river end of a post-Ford horse paddock and then doglegs back to the old rice mill, or the "laboratory" or "power plant" as it was variously known during the Ford days.

Located at the rice mill, which had been left in ruins by General Sherman and his cohorts, was the power plant for the new Richmond Hill Plantation house. A steam generator with two V-8 engine back-ups provided DC current. Upstairs from the underground power complex was the "laboratory." This was not like the special research facility of the same name to be built down in Ways. This place at the end of the tunnel was for Henry Ford himself.

A better name might have been "tinkering laboratory." In it were parts of old cars, a little steam engine and even a jewelers desk where Ford, a onetime watchmaker, periodically dabbled in his former trade.

Former research assistant in the other laboratory, Dr. Leslie Long, characterized the purpose of the rice mill laboratory:

> Mr. Ford wanted to get away from the hurly burly of Dearborn and get down here where he could think. He could escape all that pressure in his laboratory. That is the reason he liked it so well down here. It was a thinking place."

Other local employees also recalled Ford's delight with the tunnel going to the rice mill. One remembers that he liked to take nighttime walks in the lighted tunnel in his slippers and that he would often walk through it to the power plant in the mornings to greet the workers and talk politics with them. One year, during some of his "tunnel talks," he was particularly interested in finding out the opinion of the Southern working class toward Presidential candidate Wendell Wilkie.

Socially

The Richmond Hill house was never the scene of the social gatherings that were more the case at his Dearborn residence. The old photos of the "folk dances" held under the giant oaks were much more the exception than the rule. The local lore had such families as the Vanderbilts, Rockefellers and even Duponts (bitter enemies of Ford's) visiting them at Richmond Hill. Such was simply not the case.

One of the things the Fords particularly liked about their winter home was the privacy. They could move about in freedom and seldom had house guests apart from family. The Fords did have friends in Savannah and seemed to enjoy "antiquing" in the old city and visiting with them then but there appears to be no overnighting at the big house even for these neighbors. When people from Savannah did come out and spend the night or attend special functions, they were accommodated at the Cherry Hill House or occasionally at the Community House downtown.

Ford was basically a shy man who sought to avoid the stares of strangers. As a result, he usually would avoid routines when going outside of Richmond Hill to dine out or tend to other duties. One exception was Edward's Barber Shop on Bull Street in Savannah where Henry liked a young barber named Prince Ayers whom he always tipped $1.

When in Savannah, he also liked to drop in unannounced on the Mayor for a friendly chat and on the head of the City's Industrial Commission, C.C. Curtis of the Savannah Electric Company. He also would visit publisher-banker Herchel V. Jenkins who at one time told his newspaper editors to "avoid covering the routine activities of Ford so he wouldn't be discouraged from roaming about Savannah."

Clara Ford had a kindred spirit nearby in Mrs. Alethia Rotan of Philadelphia. Mrs. Rotan had bought Richard Arnold's Myrtle Grove and renamed it Folly Farms. A very wealthy woman through several marriages, Mrs. Rotan had perhaps the only other private power plant besides the Fords in the area. She had also established the first "Health Association" in Ways Station, which Ford greatly expanded.

Richmond Hill seemed to be a world apart for the Fords. They had their involvements in the community but they had their escape too. The house for their retreat was by far the most freeing and delightful of the homes they possessed. It was a breath of fresh air compared to the heavy and oppressive architecture of Fair Lane in Dearborn and it was far removed from the mental and emotional pressures that surrounded Henry in Michigan.

7
MAKING IT WORK – HIS WAY

Whether it was a lone individual, a massive multi-national integrated corporation or a 70,000 acre plantation called Richmond Hill in Georgia, Henry Ford pointed all towards the principle of self-sufficiency. He loathed the welfare concept and even when he was engaged in acts of welfare-like compassion, he was working toward the self-supporting concept.

An example on the personal level in Richmond Hill, then Ways Station, was Ford's attitude toward the local moonshiners. When Henry came to town, possibly the biggest business in the county was the illegal manufacture of liquor. Once the Ford property began to come together, its new owner asked for an inventory of stills on his property. There were approximately 250, which meant that there was almost one still per extended family being operated in that part of the county.

Marvin Sharpe was in charge of "cleaning up" the stills on Mr. Ford's property in Bryan County. After several months the temperance champion came back to town and searched out Sharpe to see how the unpopular project was going. Sharpe happily took his boss to the Cherry Hill garage and showed him around 50 stills that he had confiscated up to that time.

Ford expressed dismay that they had been so preserved and then went on to explain to Sharpe that their next order of business must be to provide work for the unemployed moonshiners. "It's not right to take away a man's livelihood without replacing it with something," said Ford.

The Saw Mill and Carpentry Shop
When Henry Ford first came to town, the local saw mill had been the major legal employer in the area. But it had fallen into disrepair so one of the first things Ford did in the community was to put it back into operation, harvest some trees and put men to work. With the lumber it produced, Ford launched into the health centers and school building program. A new, wonderful mill, by Ways Station standards, was soon built by Henry. A fire house, the two chapels and the community house were built from its products, all of which provided jobs for men who wanted them.

Soon a carpentry shop and a cabinet finishing shop were created in conjunction with the saw mill and the consolidated white school. Both black and white schools were given trade schools by Ford but the carpenter shop located near the plantation office became a real money maker and major employer. From an entrepreneurial standpoint, it was first oriented to making crates for the iceberg lettuce and other produce shipped out by Ford Farms.

Besides the church pews, kindergarten toys, school furniture and home furniture, regular products of Richmond Hill's numerous Ford-trained carpenters, the carpentry shop also made a boat. It was not just any boat. It was made for Mr. Ford who called it "Little Lulu." A 28 foot cabin cruiser, the personable little craft was the pride of the shop and the Fords as well. It was powered by two Ford V-8 engines.

The Ford Farms Research
Agricultural research was a vital ingredient in Ford's farming enterprise at Richmond Hill. Ford had the clear objective to make the plantation pay for itself but he also was always on the prowl for new products or better ways to do things that had to be done.

"Our real security is in the soil," Ford said as he walked the Richmond Hill estate in 1938. "Children ought to be taught to use their hands as well as their heads," he continued. It was a philosophy he never abandoned. The combination of head-work and hand-work in his Georgia experiment is a fascinating thing to behold.

At the helm of the "hands on" operations of his ventures stood the Scotch-Irishman J.F. (Jack) Gregory, who started with Ford in Georgia in 1925. By 1943, his operation was selling an impressive $200,000 worth of farm products for his Michigan boss.

Directing the "head-work" part of the operation, the research end, stood H.G. Ukkelberg, one of Thomas Edison's chemists and the man who had headed up the alternate rubber source research project for the Edison/Ford/Firestone consortium in Fort Myers, Florida. When Edison died in 1931, Ukkelberg and the research project were continued by Ford and Firestone in Fort Myers but in 1936 Firestone withdrew and Ford hired the chemist to continue the rubber research project at Richmond Hill.

After testing 10,000 different plants in Florida, it was goldenrod, the source of sneezes, to which Ukkelberg eventually turned as a source for rubber. The plant turned out to be one of the highest natural rubber producers of any native American species. With this discovery, Ford issued instructions that goldenrod plants be gathered from around North and South America with the result that his researcher ended up with 70 varieties to work with and around 10,000 individual plants grown and cross bred.

The leaves of the goldenrod yielded around 3% rubber naturally. The vision of Ford was to see huge fields of goldenrod glistening in the sun (dispatching tons of its allergic pollen into the winds) and great American combines rumbling up and down the rows harvesting the nation's next rubber crop.

Dusk on the Ogeechee
brings a quiet awe to
Sterling Bluff.

Henry Ford and friends are pictured outside a house he built for a poor neighbor.

RICHMOND HILL LIBRARY

The Ford team at Richmond Hill successfully made plastic from corncobs. (L-R) H.K. Ukkelberg, Ford, Jack Gregory.

By the time the project was moved to Richmond Hill, cross breeding had increased the rubber yield to around 6% and the results held promise although the rubber product cost around $2 per pound to produce. Reportedly there were 14-foot high goldenrod plants which emerged from these experiments. But alas, the withdrawal of Firestone, who had developed his own rubber source in Liberia, and the approaching Great Depression worked against the venture. Before long, development of synthetic rubber from coal and petroleum by the Germans would put an end to it.

Rice to Lettuce

Once the labors of transferring the goldenrod project to Georgia were complete, Edison's chemist could apply his talents to a major problem that was plaguing Jack Gregory. The dilemma was the old rice fields that had made Cherry Hill and Richmond plantations so prosperous in the days before the Civil War. Gregory had repaired the broken dikes that were letting the tides wash in and out and had attempted to convert these large and seemingly fertile plots from rice into iceberg lettuce.

But failure had plagued every crop. The crops simply would not grow, even in what seemed to be such ideal circumstances. Ukkelberg's research determined that the soil was woefully deficient in lime and phosphorus and once these nutrients were added in massive doses (up to 20 tons per acre), the old rice fields turned a profit for nine of the next ten years, a good record on any farm.

Promoting New Ideas

Henry Ford's general objective for the research end of the Richmond Hill farming enterprise was to find ways to convert farm products into goods usable in the auto industry. He was particularly interested in crops that could produce oils and plastics. Some 365 varieties, strains and selections of Henry's favorite crop, the soybean, were grown at Richmond Hill with an eye to its oil production.

During this time China had a worldwide monopoly on Tung oil, less an aggravation to Ford than the British control of rubber but disturbing nonetheless if for principle's sake. As a result, some 200 acres of tung trees were planted by Ukkelberg.

Ironically, the making of alcohol was reintroduced at Richmond Hill by Ford, this time from from sweet potatoes and from rice. Instead of moonshine purposes, it was blended with gasoline and used as motor fuel on the

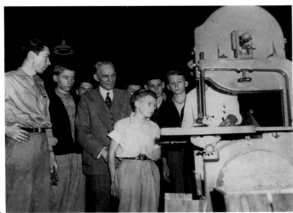

The Trade School receives a visit from its famous benefactor.

Goldenrod was a potential source of American rubber and was cultivated on the Ford Farms.

plantation. Henry was concerned about the day when sources of gasoline might run out and leave his cars and his company without power.

Ford had ways of promoting thinking and innovation among his employees. "His greatest asset was ideas," reflects Dr. Long, who also remembers his "being good to employees while ruling with an iron hand. You knew who was boss," is how Long phrased it.

When the boss got into the realm of ideas he expected action. "He liked to see results," commented H.K. Ukkelberg. "You ought to have something new every day to show me," he quotes Ford as saying. "This was kind of hard to do," concluded Ukkelberg.

Dr. Long tells the story of the time Mr. Ford dropped in on rayon specialist Frank McCall in the lab and, looking out the window, asked the researcher how many needles there might be on a certain pine.

The flabbergasted McCall was at a total loss for an answer but by the next morning he had calculated the number to be around 159,000. "Mr. Ford never asked again," said Long, "but that was the way he did things. He would ask questions to make you think about things you had never thought about before."

Sawdust Crusade

Persuaded from an early age that "wastefulness was wrong," Henry Ford always tried to find uses for things that traditionally were considered disposable. He struggled with the questions of slag waste at his Detroit factories.

At Richmond Hill the issue was sawdust from the saw mill plus bark and tree tops and waste products that result from farming such as corn cobs. One goal for the Georgia operation was to produce a type of rayon from waste products which could be used for tires, belting and upholstery.

Dr. Leslie Long, Ukkelberg's assistant who still resides on the Ogeechee Neck, remembers being at work in the research laboratory one morning when Mr. Ford and his chauffeur, Wilson, drove up at 8 A.M., both getting out of the car and opening the trunk. In the trunk were many boxes which Mr. Ford and Wilson began carrying into the lab. "In the boxes were samples of bark from every kind of tree in Richmond Hill," reported Dr. Long.

"What are you doing?" Ford asked Long.

"Determining the oil content of some soybeans," was the reply.

"Can't you stop that?" inquired Ford.

"Yes, sir," came the reply.

"I want you fellows to work full time on finding a use for this bark," instructed Mr. Ford." We are wasting tons of it every day. It must have some good use!"

"From that moment on, finding a use for that bark was our top priority," said Dr. Long. "We finally were able to make some weak plastic from it and that seemed to satisfy Mr. Ford."

By 1940, the research laboratory had come up with a process utilizing sweet gum and black gum pulp to produce rayon fiber. One tangible result was two dozen socks knitted from the rayon thread and given to Ford. Ukkelberg's assistant reported that Ford was "very proud of this and proudly wore these socks and went around pulling up his pants leg and saying, 'See that – this used to be a black gum tree.'"

All They Needed To Know

There were lots of hits and lots of misses in the Ford research operations at Richmond Hill. For the most part, the general public did not even know these sorts of things were going on.

What they saw were men working, children in perhaps some of the best schools in Georgia, quality food at the Ford Commissary, healthy families, the Ford bakery, the Ford turpentine plant, the Ford-built chapels, the Ford firehouse, the Ford-built post office, the Ford garage, the Ford school buses all over the county, the Ford laundry, the Ford blacksmith shop and the ice plant. They saw sick people being treated and even sent up to "Mr. Ford's Hospital in Detroit" at his expense when the need was justified.

They saw old people learning to read at 70 and children destined to be "moonshiners" or "fishin people" going off to college. They saw old houses being fixed and new ones built for people by Mr. Ford. They saw people like Lee Slocum being taken off the relief or WPA roles by Mr. Gregory and hired to teach a skill, basket and cane-seat weaving, to the young people of the community. They saw the reason this happened was that "Mr. Ford (the world famous billionaire) felt that a man with his technical knowledge should not be on relief." They saw what this did for Lee Slocum.

They saw Mr. Ford drive by with a friendly wave out the window of his Ford car. They saw and knew all they needed to know about Henry Ford.

8

FORD THE MAN – MYTHS AND MEMORIES

*Mr. and Mrs. Ford
loved to dance and
made sure that dancing
was taught locally.*

THE EDISON INSTITUTE, DEARBORN, MICH.

Henry Ford was a man of many pictures. Most of those painted by the world media pictured an exalted version of a human being, much like the gods of Greek mythology. No one could have lived up to the likeness regularly depicted of Henry Ford but, as in the old days of Rome and Greece, it really did not matter as people wanted to believe what they wanted to believe.

Thus the press would unreservedly report such "news stories" as that Henry was planning to spend $100 million to harness the Bay of Fundy's tide or that he would invest $120 million to produce motion pictures in behalf of blue Sundays or anti-semitism or even that he had offered to buy and scrap the entire French navy.

There seemed no end to what could be published about the allegedly limitless resources and derring-do of the incredible Henry Ford. One string of stories reported that he would give $1 million to anyone who could give him an idea that would save ten cents in manufacturing the Model T. Another reported that he had learned how to make trolley cars run on straw; another that he was developing a method to produce cars out of cotton, stamping them out like cookies.

The stock of the New York National City Bank once rose 15 points on a report that Ford was to become one of its directors and on another day the stock of Gulf States Steel Company dropped 20 points on reports that Ford was not interested in buying it. Newspaper cartoonists often drew him as a "Colossus of Transportation, " surrounded by his ships, planes, trains, tractors and cars or happily spinning the world with power supplied by his many products. That was one of the sides which the world saw of Henry Ford as presented and fabricated by the media. This was not the man who came to Richmond Hill.

Another publication, the ATLANTA JOURNAL, painted a very different picture of Henry Ford on March 17, 1945. In an article subtitled "OWNER OF VAST DOMAIN CREATED FROM OGEECHEE SWAMPS RELAXES FROM JOB," the staff reporter does a credible job of capturing a much more accurate picture of the Henry Ford seen by the people of Richmond Hill:

> RICHMOND HILL, Ga., March 17. – The 85,000 acres which comprise Richmond Hill Plantation are being visited these balmy spring days by the owner of this vast domain, 82-year old Henry Ford, whose vision has created an agricultural show place from land in many cases reclaimed from the Ogeechee River swamps by dike and channel.
>
> Mr. Ford's tall, spare figure is seen almost every day by some of the plantation's several hundred employees.
>
> He rambles through the woods near his home in perfect freedom, however, and frequently visits the various enterprises of this complete community.

> About him everywhere are the beauties of nature – tall pines, ancient moss-hung oaks and creatures of the woods, squirrels, deer and birds in profusion.
>
> ### Lost None of Genius
> Mr. Ford frequently talks with plantation employees. A workman who has charge of the electric generating plant found out the other day that the industrialist has lost none of his genius for motors.
>
> When Mr. Ford strolled into the plant he immediately noticed that the electric generator didn't sound exactly right. He cocked an ear and listened a moment, then remarked to the workman, "Something's wrong with your armature." The diagnosis was correct.
>
> The Fords customarily come here each January and remain until sometime during March.
>
> ### Place to Relax
> Here the ruler of the Ford empire can relax from his endeavors, but he maintains constant communication with Detroit. He's still the boss.
>
> ### Loved By All
> His personality has seeped into every corner of the community. At the Negro school Saturday on one of the blackboards was written this Ford-ism: "Nothing is particularly hard if you divide it into small jobs. – Henry Ford."
>
> You don't find anybody on these broad acres, beautiful now with azaleas and green carpet grass, who doesn't speak of Mr. Ford with the greatest respect. They enjoy the wave he gives them when he rides by in his Ford and they like him to view their accomplishments. He's more than a part-time citizen to a great many of the employees – he's the man who showed them a new and better way of life.

Indeed this was part of the picture of Richmond Hill's Henry Ford. But the full picture must also paint in the gadfly who kept trying to turn farm refuse into plastics or make rubber from a plant that made people sneeze or the positive thinker who would not let a little thing like malaria interfere with a good climate. There were many, many sides to Henry Ford, including that which even delighted in some of the absurd stories about him.

The Oyster House and Log Cabins
Just downriver from the powerhouse/laboratory/rice mill lies a delightful little cabin built by Henry Ford. It is a simple little structure built with precise craftsmanship, including wooden pegs, air vents and a cooking fireplace with swivel anvils and a built in baking oven. It is wonderfully rustic but not the least bit crude. A brick path approaches it from the direction of the power plant and continues on to the remains of a privy with porcelain facilities.

Veterans of the Ford era remember when the little cabin was built. "Mr. Ford had a party planned for the weekend," recalls Dr. Long, "and decided that they would have an oyster roast with Kilkenny oysters. So he told his

*The Oyster House (left)
as it looks today.*

Mrs. Ford particularly wanted a dramatic upward sweep of pillars in her Georgia mansion.

men to build him a cabin for the occasion. That was on a Tuesday with the party coming on the following Saturday."

"By the time Saturday came the cabin was there," recalls Mrs. Long, who worked in payroll. "The whole staff came down to see what the carpenters had been able to do on such short notice."

Old pictures of the just completed cabin show a sign over the door reading "AIG ROEG." No one seems to remember what it meant. A sleeping loft up some steep stairs indicates the cabin was designed for more uses than the one oyster roast that is recalled.

Henry Ford liked log cabins. He kept a log cabin in the middle of the several thousands of acres around his home and birdhouses in Dearborn and one room in his mansion was built to resemble the inside of a rustic cabin.

Ford liked an "outdoorsman" image. One cannot forget the "Vagabonds" as Thomas Edison, Harvey Firestone, John Burroughs and Henry Ford termed themselves whenever they went on one of their massively publicized outings into the woods of the Upper Peninsula or the Adirondacks of New York. Among the headlines that ran during these annual outings that begin in 1918 were "MILLIONS OF DOLLARS WORTH OF BRAINS OFF ON VACATION" and "GENIUS TO SLEEP UNDER THE STARS." President Harding even joined the foursome on one trip.

The "roughing it" facts of life, however, were more along the lines of Fair Lane's "Field Room" than the press was led to believe or at least communicated to their readers. While Henry Ford did like to chop the firewood for the foursome, each man had his own 10 x 10 tent complete with wooden floor, electricity, folding cot, mattress, blankets, sheets and pillow. Each emerged for breakfast in collar, tie and three-piece suit and an entourage of vehicles and servants accompanied the men on their "wilderness experience."

The "Vagabonds," Edison, John Burroughs, Ford and Harvey Firestone, took highly publicized camping trips together.

When first completed, the Oyster House had a sign over the door reading, "AIG ROEG."

THE EDISON INSTITUTE, DEARBORN, MICH.

Secret Doors

Local Ford mythology has arisen in Richmond Hill over reports of secret doors in bedrooms and midnight tunnel excursions by the great auto baron. Hunter Saussy, Jr., who was project engineer for the restoration of the Richmond Hill house in 1983, reports that indeed there was a secret passage in Henry Ford's closet that ran into the closet of the adjacent upstairs bedroom.

It was a sliding door that slid into the hollow of the wall but, aside from not being visible when the closet door was closed, was not very secretive in appearance. This does not well suit the local lore that relishes in stories of the roving eye credited to Ford. While there was ample reason for such stories earlier in his life, Henry was 75 years old when the Richmond Hill mansion was finished.

A far better explanation for the "secret door" is another trademark that followed Ford wherever he went. Henry hated to be cornered! Put him in a board room or an office for a meeting and he was like a caged lion. He hardly even visited his office at the Rouge plant in Michigan but holed up in a dimly lit cubbyhole in the tractor plant that had both a front and a back door, a way to slip out if he so desired.

Ford didn't like getting into cars with people he was fearful might "talk his ear off" and he hated most social gatherings for that purpose. Finally, when he would not attend any company meetings, the leadership of the company devised a system where they would get their work done with Mr. Ford over lunch and his lunches were scheduled accordingly for years.

This same principle carried over into his homes. There was always a way out, in case he got trapped by an undesirable. The tunnels played a vital part in this Ford escape mechanism. The tunnel at Richmond Hill was accessed through the basement and the only way to the basement was by the elevator.

So if he wanted to slip out of the house, he could take the elevator to the basement without encountering anybody else in the house, walk down the 1,400 foot length of the tunnel and be free; free to start rumors, free to walk out in the woods and enjoy his birds, free to talk with the old timers who hung around the Richmond Hill power plant at the other end of the tunnel and free to tinker in his personal laboratory.

The sliding door in the closet? Probably a final way to get out without anyone knowing, an "escape hatch." There was even a "secret" exit from the little log cabin down by the river. To the left of the fireplace, what seems like a narrow stretch of wall, perhaps 4 feet wide, is hinged from the outside and simply pushes out and becomes an exit. There are no knobs or anything else to give the appearance of a door.

These escape devices reflect upon who Henry Ford was and why he came to Richmond Hill in the first place. He was one of the most important, powerful, wealthy and therefore sought after people in the world during his day. He liked to call press conferences but he did not like to be summoned to them or trapped into them, whether at the White House, his office in Dearborn or at home in his winter retreat in Georgia.

The Fords loved Richmond Hill because of the privacy it provided and because they were seen differently by the people who lived there. They were not "locked in" at Richmond Hill as they were elsewhere, Mrs. Ford once commented. She delighted that they were able to move about in safety and without the publicity which leaving the house usually entailed. It was often said, along the banks of the Ogeechee, that Mr. Ford had the appearance of being a boy again as he darted happily about his multitudinous projects in the community and on the plantation.

Clara Ford

Clara Ford was not as visible at Richmond Hill as her husband. She took a personal interest in the schools and the more extreme housing needs of some of the people. She went with Henry to the dances at the Community House and looked in on the chapel service from time to time. And she had a far greater influence on her husband than we will probably ever know.

The Fords had a delightful little ritual that took place whenever the breadwinner arrived home. He would swing open the door of Fair Lane or Richmond Hill and give out a birdlike warble to let Clara know he was home and she would return the call, letting him know that she was home herself.

Even when lounging on the steps of his plantation house, Ford wore his familiar three-piece suit.

43

The Yacht Basin of the Fords as it exists today. Here the Little Lulu was berthed.

Clara was a frugal woman, still the farmer's wife. As a result she used to do certain things that would drive Henry Ford to distraction. One was darning socks.

Clara had darned Henry's socks in their days of comparative poverty and did not see why she should stop since they now had a bit of money. She insisted on darning Henry's socks even though there was nothing in the world he detested more than a darned sock. It was a situation with an impasse. But Henry was the one who blinked.

Ford confidante and long-time employee Harry Bennett tells of the numerous times that he was driving Ford through Dearborn and the boss would motion him to a men's store and pause long enough to buy some new socks. "Then he would change in the car, tossing the pair Mrs. Ford had so carefully darned out the window," Bennett reported. "The spectacle of a man with a billion dollars changing socks in his car so his wife wouldn't know about it was, at least," said Bennett, "a unique one."

Mrs. Ford made a lot of people blink. "Mrs. Ford was a character," recalls Dr. Long. "People always tried to be out of the way when she came around." Long's boss, Harry Ukkelberg, gave a newspaper interview where he recalled a foreman hiding a worker who had fallen into disfavor with Mrs. Ford to keep him from being fired. Ukkelberg himself sometimes got summoned by Mrs. Ford to the mansion.

> "Tell you the truth, I just hated to go," commented the researcher. "But once we had a good time. She wanted to lay a brick walk. I don't know why she called me, since she had two bricklayers sitting there.
>
> "But Mrs. Ford was particular about the curve of her walk and the quaking bricklayers did not measure up.
>
> "So the both of us got down on our hands and knees and sited those stakes. Oh, she was in a good humor that day."

One of Mrs. Ford's loves of Richmond Hill was her rose garden. She had a garden of greatly prized roses and a massive Lady Bankshire climbing rose on one corner of the house. Many of the early pictures of the house have that 20 foot rose in the background.

Mrs. Ford was very particular about her flowers. She always insisted on having King Alfred jonquils, blue violets, gladiolus and pansies blooming when the family arrived. A greenhouse managed by Ukkelberg helped nature to cooperate. "Now you better have them when Mrs. Ford arrived," was the researcher's summation of his gardening duties.

The early pictures also show tricycles and children. These belonged to the great grandchildren of the Fords, Ann and Charlotte, children of Henry Ford II who himself reportedly only visited Richmond Hill once. Son Edsel visited and his youngest two children, William Clay and Josephine, also spent time at their grandparents' winter home.

The Ford yacht basin holds a special remembrance of the Ford grandchildren. Henry took a morning constitutional walk there daily from the mansion accompanied by Wilson, his chauffeur. Besides berthing "Little Lulu," it was used as a swimming pool by the Ford clan and for at least one employee party.

Somewhere in the concrete steps that provide pool-like access to the fluctuating tidal water of the basin, are little hand prints. The final concrete work was being done while the youngsters were in residence and the Ford children were like any other children. They could not resist the urge so somewhere in the basin, awaiting rediscovery, are the tiny handprints of those famous Ford youngsters.

Change in the Air

There was always an air of excitement when the Fords were in residence during those years. The personal enthusiasm, the always probing mind and manner of Henry Ford seemed to permeate everywhere. The excitement seemed to even peak just before the family arrived.

Fifty additional people were usually hired by Jack Gregory to look after the extra sprucing up that would be required before the Fords arrived. The grounds would receive special treatment. Mrs. Ford's flower garden would be finely managed and fresh flowers cut and arranged for the house. All the Ford buildings and operations would be brought to the expected level of neatness and special research projects would be brought to the point where they would pass Mr. Ford's close inspection. He had a reputation of being fast of foot and was apt to show up unexpectedly with lots of pointed questions.

Actually, the whole year had become exciting in Richmond Hill. The Ford trucks would rumble back and forth between Dearborn and Georgia transporting cement from the North and if prior to a Ford visit, favorite kitchen goods, books, phonograph records and other items needed for the visit.

During the year a steady flow of items was shipped North including shad from the Ogeechee, fresh fruits and vegetables, figs, and grapes from Mrs. Ford's vines. During Christmas, mistletoe, holly, pecans, sweet potatoes and cured hams would leave Richmond Hill for Fair Lane. These were active, exciting years.

With the approach of World War II the pace would slow as Henry Ford became increasingly occupied with turning out war material for the allies. "Little Lulu" was marshalled into the coastal defense forces by the Coast Guard and the flow of trucks and equipment to Georgia slowed and even stopped as national priorities were elsewhere. It was the beginning of the end for the Ford era at Sterling Bluff.

9
THE TRANSITIONAL YEARS

THE EDISON INSTITUTE, DEARBORN, MICH.

The Fords would occasionally bring an orchestra down from Michigan to play for dances on their lawn.

The gardens around the plantation house have been even further expanded by the Pharaons.

What had taken place at Richmond Hill for almost two decades could not go on, nor should it. A community with such historic vitality as that possessed by the Ogeechee Neck once again had to find its feet and begin to function on its own.

Bryan County and Richmond Hill had known glorious years. It had also known the sad chapters of being decimated by war and its aftermath. Now it had been remarkably stirred by Mister Ford and shades of glory began to return. There had to come a post-Ford era and the long view would prove that it would be for the best.

Still the transition period of moving from grateful dependence on the Michigan benefactor to life increasingly absent of his familiar influence, was painful and sad. It did not happen suddenly but mercifully took place over a full decade. The process began with World War II.

1941
It was the same year that World War II began to seriously affect the operation of Richmond Hill Plantation. Several hundred acres were taken by the Army for Fort Stewart. The next year the Coast Guard would requisition the Fords' personable cabin cruiser, "Little Lulu," for patrol duty in the inland waterways. Somehow it was like the family's youngest daughter going off to war.

The year 1941 was also when H.G. Ukkelberg made plastic tiles for Ford from corn cobs in his research laboratory. It was also the year that Ukkelberg's research laboratory burned, Henry Ford being advised of disaster by telegram at 2:55 P.M. September 22 : "LABORATORY BURNED SATURDAY MORNING. NOTHING SAVED BUT RECORDS. WILL CALL YOU IN MORNING. J.F. GREGORY."

The sad reply came back from Dearborn: "DO NOT UNDER ANY CIRCUMSTANCES REBUILD LABORATORY."

The Effects of the War
During the war years, the influence and the presence of the Fords waned in Richmond Hill. Government regulations made the operation of the Ford facilities increasingly difficult. The flow of cars, trucks and tractors from Michigan slowed to a trickle.

Mr. and Mrs. Ford still made trips to their beloved Richmond Hill but the trips were shorter in duration and more infrequent. Henry continued to delight in the talks at the end of the tunnel at the power plant. He liked to tell the story of his visit with President Wilson in 1915. The President and Henry Ford had been at odds over Henry's ill-advised peace initiative but politics and public relations had brought them together for a much publicized meeting at the White House in November of that year.

Henry Ford especially loved the local children and these (circa. 1935) clearly enjoyed him as well.

THE EDISON INSTITUTE, DEARBORN, MICH.

Ford made a habit of hiring handicapped people such as Will Shamus.

Fine Arabian horses now live on the Sterling Bluff Plantation grounds. (right)

THE EDISON INSTITUTE, DEARBORN, MICH.

Ford would relate how he had done his best to put the President at ease by sitting with one leg over the arm of his chair and telling him the latest Ford joke about the man who asked to be buried in his Model T because it had pulled him out of every other hole he had been in. This had apparently caused the President to respond with a limerick but the good natured time in the public glare ultimately produced little but some enjoyable memories.

Other Changes

In the spring of 1945 Henry Ford suffered a significant stroke and during that year turned the reins of the Ford Motor Company over to grandson Henry Ford II. The stroke, actually his second, was not publicized but the effects impacted the already dwindling operations in Georgia. The overseeing of Richmond Hill fell to Mrs. Ford and from then on, a different spirit characterized the plantation. A confidential appraisal of the Georgia operations was ordered and a mandate given to drastically reduce expenses.

Clara and Henry Ford made their last trip together to Richmond Hill early in the spring of 1947. The azaleas were in bloom and the spring flowers were popping through in Mrs. Ford's gardens. The grounds were not

Former switchboard operator for Ford operations, Margaret Fennell, still lives in Richmond Hill.

as immaculate as they had been in years past but they were still acceptable. Clara was more tolerant of such things and Henry just was not noticing any more.

Age and the stroke had caught up with the sharp-minded Ford. There were times that he was the Henry of old but, more than likely, he was confused and missed a lot of what was being said. Clara was in charge of things except when Henry was in one of his sharper stages or when his brusque nature would erupt.

Marvin Sharpe remembers Ford's last days at Richmond Hill. He remembered him sitting at his favorite place in the rice mill looking out the window at the men working. He would talk about "the days gone by," said Sharpe. But toward the end "you could tell he was not nearly as active.

"He didn't go to the rice mill.
He didn't go to the tunnel.
He didn't go over the plantation much.
You didn't see him out around the roses.
He didn't fool around with his clocks or tinker like he used to.
He didn't sit and chat with you as long as he used to.
He didn't ask many questions."

Home to Dearborn

The Fords returned to Dearborn from their annual Richmond Hill migration on Easter Sunday, April 6. The next day, the man who had revolutionized world industry was dead. He was 83 years old.

There was a service in Richmond Hill for Henry Ford at the same time his funeral service was being held in the massive Detroit Cathedral with thousands standing outside. The people of Richmond Hill met in the Martha-Mary Chapel with its sharp white steeple.

In Detroit, Ford was eulogized as a great inventor and producer. He had "revolutionized American and world industry," they said.

In Richmond Hill people like Margaret Fennel would remember him differently. "He was just as common as we were," she said. "You would never know he was a millionaire. He changed my life. I was from a very poor family and the values he instilled in me are still with me today."

That was the way most people remember Henry Ford on that sad day in Richmond Hill. To them, to those who knew him on the Ogeechee Neck, Henry Ford was, above everything else, a friend. Now their friend was gone.

10
THE ERA OF
GHAITH PHARAON

The will of Henry Ford left the entirety of his holdings, minus Clara's dream house, to the Ford Foundation. In 1942 the property was appraised at around $3 million. Mrs. Ford indicated that she would like to see the forest and farming operations continued for the good of the people and so they were until Mrs. Ford's death in September 1950, the same year that the household furnishings from the mansion were shipped back to Dearborn.

The coup de grâce to Ford operations in Bryan County came on May 11, 1951 when the sawmill burned. It had been exactly ten years and ten days since the festive day when Ways Station was renamed Richmond Hill. The old order had changed during that time.

After the fire, Benson Ford announced the complete discontinuance of local Ford operations in a letter to the remaining local employees. All company affairs were subsequently tidied up. The Ford era was over.

Post Ford

These were not easy years for Richmond Hill but they provided the time required for the community to re-establish its own unique identity. Today the town and Bryan County are thriving and in the first of a growth boom. The Ogeechee Neck is a vital place to live and the people are proud of their substantial heritage.

It was not a simple matter to decide what to do with the Ford holdings. After all, they amounted to around 70,000 acres and more than 170 structures. And there simply were not any more Henry Fords out there, not even in Michigan, not even in the Ford Foundation. There were no other candidates to fill his shoes.

What finally happened was that the Ford assets in Bryan County ended up with International Paper Company, which was primarily interested in the still substantial timber assets. Along with the trees, for a reported price of $5 million, went the 170 or so structures, houses and in essence, the village of Richmond Hill. International Paper proceeded to divest itself of being a landlord as best it could while holding on to the timber and other real estate assets.

Ford-owned houses were sold to those who would buy them. In 1958 Fort McAllister was given to the State of Georgia and is now operated by the Georgia Department of Natural Resources, Parks Division. In 1959, Henry Ford's mansion on the Ogeechee along with 1,200 acres was sold to a New Hampshire industrialist. Over the next ten years that property changed hands three times with various schemes and plans for the elegant estate put forth. The house was converted into a restaurant at one point, with the surrounding gardens and gracious lawn asphalted over for parking but the enterprise failed a year later. At one point the mansion was actually used to store hay.

The Ford mansion today (left) with the elegant gardens carrying on the Fords' rose garden heritage.

Sand and water protect the approach to the second hole at Sterling Bluff.

The grassed entry road to Sterling Bluff circles this fountain before providing access to the mansion.

New Vitality Comes with The Eighties

The eighth decade of the twentieth century brought a stability and prosperity to Bryan County and Richmond Hill that it had not experienced since before the War Between the States. It had been around 120 years since the destruction of the Ogeechee Breadbasket but at last the area was once again getting its own bearings. The Ford years had brought back a degree of those glorious years but now there was an important difference. There was no single personage or institution which could pull the rug out from under the community or the economy should they depart.

Also in the eighties, the "right" person came along for Henry Ford's plantation house. He was a man with a number of Henry Ford-like qualities yet very different at the same time.

Ghaith R. Pharaon

Ghaith R. Pharaon purchased the Ford Mansion and 1,800 acres in 1981 and set to work restoring the plantation house while making plans to move his American business headquarters to Richmond Hill. Also included in the acreage were Cherry Hill Plantation, the site of the Silk Hope Plantation, and a portion of the Sterling Bluff Plantation estate settled by the Scottish brothers William and Hugh Sterling in 1734.

For two and a half centuries this property has been sought by and has fallen in and out of the hands of adventurers, the lords of the plantations and the premier industrialists of the world. Now one of the most prominent international entrepreneurs of this generation has become lord of this historic estate.

An aerial view shows the delightful relationship between the historic plantation house site and Ogeechee River.

Though familiar with virtually all corners of the world, Pharaon saw the beauty and tranquility in Sterling Bluff that so intrigued Henry and Clara Ford. In it Pharaon also saw, "the ultimate retreat, one offering beauty, splendor and serenity."

Pharaon spent much of his youth in Europe where his father, Dr. Rachad Pharaon, served as the Saudi Arabian ambassador to all of Europe from 1948 to 1953. From 1953 until 1980 Dr. Pharaon served as Minister and Chief Advisor to every Saudi Arabian king. The younger Pharaon was educated in France during his primary years and thereafter in Lebanon, Syria and Switzerland. His university education was in the United States with degrees from the Colorado School of Mines, Stanford University and an MBA from Harvard. He owns homes in Paris, London, Jeddah, Cannes, a castle in the Dordogne at Montfort in France, and other secondary residences in the Far East, such as Hong Hong and Labuan on the island of Borneo.

The new occupant of the magnificent house overlooking the Ogeechee is like its famous predecessor in that his business interests are remarkably varied; nowhere among them, however, is found automobile manufacturing. Pharaon's American business involvements are managed under Inter-Redec, which is now headquartered in the old rice mill that Henry Ford converted into his power station and personal research laboratory and which Pharaon completely remodeled into offices overlooking the river.

The elegant Ford mansion overlooking the Ogeechee is now on the U.S. Department of Interior National Register of Historic Places. One of the first things Pharaon did after purchasing the estate was to initiate a complete restoration of the grand old house and to restore the mansion and enhance the grounds. No stone was left unturned and Pharaon himself devoted substantial time and energy to the task.

Every one of the approximately 500 window panes was replaced with beveled plate glass. The pine wood parquet flooring was refurbished, the exterior brickwork returned to flawless condition. Natural marble now replaces the broad terrazzo steps leading to the entry.

On the river side of the house, a large pool with a black bottom to reflect the sky has been added. In the center of the pool stands Gazzeri's 1860 marble sculpture of "The Lovers." In the front, a pair of large ornamental iron gates rescued from a New Orleans mansion have been installed, to give a sense of entry. Gardens with life-sized statuary and fountains have been created. Stables for Arabian stallions and Argentinian Polo ponies were installed. Pharaon found the original layout odd in that it placed the first floor bathrooms facing the river. In the new layout, the bathrooms were moved to less noble views. Otherwise, the original layouts of the house were strictly respected.

A white egret pauses during its fishing expedition on the banks of the Ogeechee River.

A massive oak (Overleaf) provides a dramatic target for the across-the-water approach to the eighth green.

The original marina constructed by Henry Ford for his personal yacht is being rehabilitated to accommodate the yachts of friends visiting the Pharaons from the river side.

Sterling Bluff was selected for the 1987 Award of Merit, presented annually by the American Association of Nurserymen. The award for planning and landscape architecture was given under the name of River Oaks Plantation, the original name of the Ford home.

Henry's carriage house has been enlarged and his cherished old rice mill restored and expanded to accommodate the InterRedec offices. The Cherry Hill Plantation house, which was occasionally occupied by the Fords and which continued to serve their accompanying Dearborn retinue once the mansion was in place, has been moved and rebuilt. It now serves as guest quarters once again and sits overlooking the first tee of a magnificent golf course built on the grounds. Now it is American and international guests and associates of Pharaon who marvel at the natural beauty and history of this Southern plantation.

The Sterling Bluff Golf Course

One new addition Pharaon has brought to the Ogeechee Neck area is a golf course. Although private, it is of world-class caliber and designed by Pete and P.B. Dye, renowned as the most creative golf course architects in the world.

What the Dyes do is unquestionably superb, but it can often be controversial in certain golfing circles, as they like to step beyond the "conventional" in the golf design realm. Ghaith Pharaon himself has a touch of that, having been described as a "blending of Middle Eastern tradition with the contemporary realities of Harvard Business School and the world of international finance."

The building of such a global course at Sterling Bluff is an interesting story in itself, because golf is not the passion of its owner. Pharaon personally gravitates to skiing and boating for recreation but after purchasing Sterling Bluff, he became captivated by the beauty of a course in the Dominican Republic, the renowned Casa de Campo at La Romana.

Observing the popularity of golf in America, particularly in the Southeast, where many of the best known courses are located, he decided to have a spectacular, unique course built at Sterling Bluff for his friends and guests. He wanted it to be in the tradition of the Augusta National course. After considering the world's best course designers, Pharaon settled on the Dyes because of their high level of creativity. He liked their artistic approach to design and their practice of conceptualizing, creating and contouring as they go as opposed to designing by engineering blueprints.

Pharaon was impressed by the honors which have been accorded the Dyes as a result of their great sensitivity for the natural landscape. That was good news for the historic land of the Harns and the Maxwells. GOLF DIGEST MAGAZINE, generally accepted as the best judge of the world's golf courses, has placed eight of Dye's courses on its "Top 100 Golf Courses in 1988" list. Included are such golfing household names as the Tournament Players Club at Sawgrass (Stadium Course), Ponte Vedra, Florida; Harbour Town Links and the Long Cove Club, both on nearby Hilton Head Island in South Carolina; and Oak Tree Golf Club in Edmond, Oklahoma, site of the 1988 PGA Championship.

The Dyes are a golfing family. Wife Alice, herself a full-fledged member of the American Society of Golf Course Architects, was co-designer with Pete on many courses and designed the landscape around the Sterling Bluff course. Son P.B. worked with his father on the Honors Course and Long Cove and was co-designer with him at Sterling Bluff.

One does start to wonder at what a remarkable course like Sterling Bluff is doing in a peaceful, non-resort place like Richmond Hill. But then the whole Henry Ford saga floods back once again. Henry could have gone anywhere in the world he pleased, yet he chose to come to the Ogeechee Neck. Ghaith Pharaon, the man who lives in his house now when he comes to the United States, had the same options. They both just liked it there, that's all.

Henry Ford delighted in the past and the same can be said of the Pharaons and the Dyes. They have enormous respect for heritage and time-tested formulas of success. One of the things that characterizes the Dyes as golf course design iconoclasts is their desire to return the game to some of its nineteenth century concepts, particularly in the quest of natural qualities.

In giving the Dyes the assignment to build an exemplary course here, Pharaon did not try to tell them what to do. The only instructions, according to the Dyes, were the words, "Give me a truly inspirational golfing experience that may encourage me to take up golf some day." From Pharaon's standpoint, he had "entrusted to the Dyes a commission to sculpture and create, in the tradition of an European Renaissance painter, a work of art and to use as much as 1,200 acres for their canvas."

An average golf course occupies 150 acres. The course at Sterling Bluff occupies 261. In addition, 248 acres of lakes have been created for the course.

The Dyes' choice of land at Sterling Bluff was typically unconventional. It was partially predictable, partially shocking. The front nine is a classic Dye exercise in strategic golf. It plays through a forest of pine, oak and palmetto, using tactical elements such as immense oaks, hills, swales, bunkers and large lakes to give the golfer special challenges on every hole.

The most startling feature of the golf course is that wholly half of it was built right into the middle of the ante-bellum Cherry Hill rice fields. Henry Ford turned those fields into lettuce fields, but the Dyes have added

A combination reflecting pool and swimming pool now stands on the river side of the plantation house.

1.2 million cubic yards of earth that will make it become, in all likelihood, one of the most photographed courses in America. They have made those nine holes a virtual island of Scottish moors.

The old original rice dikes still control the flow of water as they did before the Revolutionary War, leaving these truly surprising nine holes completely surrounded by two dramatic expanses of water. First come the flooded rice fields outside of the course, then the ancient rice dikes, and finally the Ogeechee River that does an ox-bow bend around the rice fields that have become golf holes. This course cannot but become one of the finest in the South.

A Final Look

As The View From Sterling Bluff focuses on today and the years ahead, the vista is exciting. It features a happy ending to some of the sad and painful chapters from earlier this century. The people of the Neck are back on their feet and looking to the future with confidence.

The new generation on the Ogeechee Neck promises to be of a stock that will not only carry its load in the community, but will preserve the heritage that has given this area its strong roots. They will remember men like Pete Rose, the Moravian game keeper who took those shots at the bear charging his party at Sterling Bluff from what is now Ford's Island. They will look back with special delight on the likes of John Harn, who established Dublin Plantation and carved order out of the same wilderness that Henry Ford tamed again in this century.

The many men of mettle who first came to the shores of the Ogeechee still provide inspiration in these days. The Indian traders, the military men like Strathy Hall's Captain Mackey, who helped subdue the Spanish threat from Florida, the idealists like James Oglethorpe – all came together to fashion the early character of the place.

The name of Jonathan Bryan remains – the old friend of liberty taken captive by the British in his 66th year. The Habersham name is remembered, too, the father for his loyalty to the Crown, his three sons as "liberty boys" who captured the Royal Governor and sent pirated gunpowder to the Boston patriots. Memories of both zealous Patriots and character-rich Tories like John Maxwell of Richmond Plantation stir the hearts of those who walk where they walked.

Then there was Colonel John White of the Georgia Continental Line, who, with seven evacuees, captured 141 British soldiers, two privateers, a sloop of 14 guns and another with 10 guns by building fires all around their foes and putting on the airs of a thousand-man force.

Colonel Anderson, CSA and Major Kilpatrick, USA played out an especially painful drama at the sandy rebel fort named after the McAllisters.

The cruelty of Sherman and his men, who had a job to do, are part of the story, too, as are the slave masters who oversaw the servile thousands who made the rice and cotton industries work on the Neck. Some might want to forget parts of these chapters but they contain important lessons. And we should remember the illiterate freed slaves and their descendants who turned out for Mr. Ford's night reading classes in such numbers, because they wanted to be able to read the Bible for themselves.

Of all those who have had an impact on the view from Sterling Bluff, none exceed that of the man from Michigan. The aura of Henry Ford lives on in Richmond Hill. Now, over four decades later, not everyone in town has his facts right about the Ford era, but deep respect for Henry and his days in rural Georgia still abounds.

And future generations will remember today and the impact of Ghaith Pharaon on these historic lands. He will be remembered for preserving much of what went before, for anchoring his American financial and industrial network on the Ogeechee Neck and, of course, for commissioning Pete and P.B. Dye to weave their golfing tapestry in the old Cherry Hill rice fields and among the ancient oaks of Sterling Bluff Plantation.

So the current View From Sterling Bluff closes. The people in the View have been as fascinating as they have been different. They repeatedly have shown a quality of character that this Ogeechee River country seems to attract. Each has been affected by that river in profound ways. And so it will doubtless continue in the future as new generations take their place in the View From Sterling Bluff.

The fifth tee at Sterling Bluff is one of the most imaginative ever created by Pete Dye.

WITH GRATITUDE
FROM THE AUTHOR

A host of people have played a part in making this book possible, and as many as possible are recalled below with thanksgiving. Particularly appreciated were the efforts of Ford Bryan, an authority on Henry Ford and Richmond Hill, who is associated with the Edison Institute Library in Dearborn, Michigan. Also very helpful at the Institute were David Crippen, Director of Archives, and Cynthia Reed-Miller, who manages the vast photographic resources of the Institute. Joan Klintoch helped keep track of the many orders placed for prints.

In Richmond Hill itself, Dr. and Mrs. Leslie Long were of great assistance, lending of their time and personal memorabilia for these pages. Dr. Long is hereby encouraged to write his own recollections of the Ford days at Richmond Hill before more fascinating chapters of the story are lost. Similar encouragements are given to Margaret Fennell, who, like Dr. Long, has been of special help. The author is also indebted to Professor John Duncan of Armstrong State University who, with Mr. Bryan and Dr. Long, reviewed manuscripts before printing. An authority on Savannah history, Dr. Duncan kept me as honest about the history of the area as Ford Bryan did about Henry Ford.

Dan Brown, Superintendent of Fort McAllister, and Mary Worsham helped with that part of the story, and Hunter Sausey, Jr., the engineer for the restoration of the Ford Mansion, provided needed assistance there. Kay Gilette, Richmond Hill librarian, Cathy Gregory, Principal Francis Meeks, Mrs. C.M. Jones, Cathy Wood, Mr. and Mrs. Jack Phillips, Mike Conner, Rod Gragg, Tom Gardo, Tim Doughtie, Bill Littell, and the Savannah Library are others who provided assistance.

A very special word of appreciation and place of admiration needs to be set aside for Will Weems, son of photographer Bill Weems. Will played an invaluable role in not only coordinating his late father's material for the book but in serving as personal guide and assistant to Steve Uzzell when he journeyed to Georgia to complete the shoot for his fallen comrade.

Gratitude certainly deserves to be extended to the InterRedec team who sparked the telling of this important story. Dr. Pharaon himself initiated the work, ably assisted by Amer Lodhi, Patricia Jacobs and David Pearson of Pearson, McGuire Associates of Coral Gables, Florida. David's encouragement has been particularly appreciated as have the labors of Ana Castilla in his office. Debbie Cumptson, of Elite Secretarial Systems of Hilton Head, typed the manuscript, often evidencing the skill of a UN interpreter. Jordan Barrett and Associates of Miami have done an excellent job in design and layout.

Finally, a special thanks to my family – my wife Ginny and children Skye and Joy – for their support as well as toleration of manuscripts and research often competing for space at the dining room table. Thanks, too, for my parents who years ago encouraged the development of communication skills and whose appreciation of history made the exploration of *The View from Sterling Bluff* an adventure.